CHURCH LIFE IN KENT
1559-1565

Also by Arthur J. Willis

CANTERBURY MARRIAGE LICENCES 1751-1780
CANTERBURY MARRIAGE LICENCES 1781-1809
CANTERBURY MARRIAGE LICENCES 1810-1837
CANTERBURY LICENCES (GENERAL) 1568-1646
HAMPSHIRE MARRIAGE LICENCES 1607-1640
HAMPSHIRE MARRIAGE LICENCES 1669-1680
HAMPSHIRE MARRIAGE ALLEGATIONS 1698-1837 (SUPPLEMENT)
WILLS, ADMINISTRATIONS AND INVENTORIES WITH THE
   WINCHESTER DIOCESAN RECORDS
WINCHESTER SETTLEMENT PAPERS 1667-1842
WINCHESTER GUARDIANSHIPS after 1700
WINCHESTER ORDINATIONS
   I Ordinands' Papers 1734-1827
   II Bishops' Registers, Subscription Books and Exhibition of Orders 1660-1829
A HAMPSHIRE MISCELLANY
   I Metropolitical Visitation 1607-8
   II Laymens' Licences of the Diocese of Winchester 1675-1834
   III Dissenters' Meeting House Certificates 1702-1844
   IV Exhibit Books, Terriers and Episcopatus Redivivus
WINCHESTER CONSISTORY COURT DEPOSITIONS (Selections 1561-1602)

and in collaboration with A.L.Merson
A CALENDAR OF SOUTHAMPTON APPRENTICESHIP REGISTERS 1609-1740
   (Southampton Records Series)

and in collaboration with Margaret J.Hoad and Robert P.Grime
BOROUGH SESSIONS PAPERS 1653-1688
   (Portsmouth Record Series)

GENEALOGY FOR BEGINNERS
INTRODUCING GENEALOGY

WORKING UP A BILL OF QUANTITIES
SOME NOTES ON TAKING OFF QUANTITIES
TO BE A SURVEYOR
AN EXAMPLE IN QUANTITY SURVEYING

and in collaboration with Christopher J.Willis
ELEMENTS OF QUANTITY SURVEYING
MORE ADVANCED QUANTITY SURVEYING
PRACTICE AND PROCEDURE FOR THE QUANTITY SURVEYOR
SPECIFICATION WRITING FOR ARCHITECTS AND SURVEYORS

and in collaboration with W.N.B.George and Christopher J.Willis
THE ARCHITECT IN PRACTICE

CHURCH LIFE IN KENT

being

Church Court Records of the Canterbury Diocese

1559-1565

by

ARTHUR J. WILLIS, F.R.I.C.S., F.S.G.

PHILLIMORE
LONDON AND CHICHESTER

Published by
PHILLIMORE & CO. LTD.
London and Chichester
Head Office: Shopwyke Hall,
Chichester, Sussex, England

© Arthur J. Willis, 1975

ISBN 0 85033 202 8

Printed by Unwin Brothers Ltd.,
Old Woking, Surrey

TABLE OF CONTENTS

	PREFACE	vii
I	INTRODUCTION	1
II	THE CLERGY	8
III	CHURCH BUILDINGS AND PRECINCTS	16
IV	CHURCH FITTINGS AND FURNISHINGS	18
V	LAYMEN AND THE CHURCH	22
VI	DISCIPLINING OF PRIVATE LIVES	41

APPENDICES
- 1. Volumes used for this book — 67
- 2. Headings of the Queen's Injunctions of 1559 — 68
- 3. Analysis of clergy 1559-1561 — 70
- 4. Directions to the clergy 1561 — 71
- 5. Analysis of detecta 1560 — 72
- 6. Visitation Articles for exempt parishes 1564 — 75
- 7. Some extracts from contemporary statutes — 76
- 8. Some rubrics of the Book of Common Prayer of 1552 — 81
- 9. A sentence of excommunication — 83

INDEXES
- Surnames — 85
- Places — 90
- Subjects — 93

PLATES
- 1. A page of a liber cleri — facing 64
- 2. A page of detecta with the action taken on them — facing 65

PREFACE

In examining the list of extant diocesan records at Canterbury it occurred to me that the records of the first few years of the reign of Elizabeth I might give an interesting picture of the ecclesiastical side of life at the change from the days of Catholic Queen Mary. Whilst they are of one diocese only, similar conditions must have prevailed throughout the country.

My first intention was to make a full calendar of the causes on the disciplinary side of the diocesan jurisdiction for the first two or three years of the reign of Elizabeth I. I did, in fact, complete this in typescript, but, feeling that its scope was not wide enough, I decided that I must include a few more years.* The cost of doing this in the form of a complete calendar would have been prohibitive, so I have extracted some of the 'meat' from it, extended to 1565, for this volume.

The disadvantage of an extract of this sort is that it does not indicate the relative extent of each type of offence. To help meet this I have made in an appendix an analysis of the causes in the first volume *(X.1.2.)* covering 1560.

In presenting this source material for historians I must emphasise that I am neither a historian nor an expert palaeographer. Chance gave me the opportunity to spend a considerable time in sorting and listing the Winchester diocesan records before they passed into the charge of the County Archivist. This, besides providing practice in deciphering the script, acquainted me with the 'doggy' Latin of the ecclesiastical courts (fortunately I started adult life as an alleged classical scholar) and at the same time developed an interest in the subject matter.

Nevertheless, it will be realised by those who have seen documents of this type that writing, particularly of notes made at a Visitation or Court, is often so scribbled as to remain a puzzle. I am very grateful to Miss Anne Oakley, archivist of the Cathedral Library for help in deciphering some of the scrawls, but there are still some undeciphered.

I am also indebted to Mr E.G.W.Bill, Librarian of Lambeth Palace Library, for identifying some of the contemporary or earlier publications to which I have referred.

The plates are reproduced by permission of the Dean and Chapter of Canterbury.

---

* This calendar (1559-1565) is available for reference at the Canterbury Cathedral Library.

'. . . these dusty records, the more poignant and strangely satisfying because it is the lives of men dead these hundreds of years, whose eyes we yet look into . . .'.

A.L. Rowse, *The England of Elizabeth*

INTRODUCTION

Everybody knows that the accession of Elizabeth I put an end to the romanizing interruption which the Reformation suffered in the reign of Mary. The Visitations of parishes by ecclesiastical authority in the first few years of Elizabeth's reign not only show the changes in personnel, they throw light on the wider sphere of social life, so much of which was subject to the discipline of the Church.

In the Canterbury Cathedral Library are deposited the early records for the administration of the diocese of Canterbury transferred from the Diocesan Registry. Amongst these are the Visitation Books and records of consequent disciplinary action taken by the two authorities - the Archdeacon and the Commissary, the latter a lawyer acting on behalf of the Archbishop, the diocesan. The Archdeacon, too, would not normally conduct these investigations personally but would have an 'Official', like the Commissary a lawyer. In both cases the Visitation might be conducted by a deputy or 'surrogate' duly appointed.

A list of the volumes used in preparation of this book is set out in Appendix 1.

AREA OF JURISDICTION. The jurisdiction here covered is limited to the diocese of Canterbury, which comprised all Kent east of a line running approximately north and south on the west side of the parishes of Rainham, Boxley, Maidstone, Marden and Goudhurst to the Sussex border. Kent west of that line was in the diocese of Rochester. The area was covered almost entirely by small villages, the only sizeable towns being Canterbury and Maidstone with Dover and Faversham approaching them and all, of course, very much smaller than they are today. The picture, then, is largely of village life, village scandal and village quarrels.

WORKING OF THE COURTS. It is not proposed to describe here the working of these courts. Any reader not acquainted with the procedure should refer to other books on the subject.* The records here are all

---

* See, for instance, 'The Consistory Court of the Diocese of Gloucester' by F.S. Hockaday (Bristol & Gloucester Archaeological Society Transactions (1924), vol. 46, p.195); 'An Introduction to Ecclesiastical Records' by Rev. J.S. Purvis (1953); or, for a quickly read thumbnail sketch, 'Winchester Consistory Court Depositions 1561-1602' by Arthur J. Willis (1960), which includes some extracts and a bibliography of other books and papers on the subject. A later useful book is 'The Records of the Established Church of England' by Dorothy M. Owen (1970), pp. 31-45.

CHURCH LIFE IN KENT

office ('ex officio') causes, i.e. causes on the disciplinary side of the jurisdictions. The 'instance' causes (which might be called the civil side as against the criminal) included such matters as testamentary, matrimonial and tithe disputes, payment of levies for church repairs or for the poor, etc., contested faculties for seating, memorials etc. and other cases which were not a sin in the eyes of the Church but were subject to ecclesiatical law. Slander was also normally a matter for personal action, though a few cases appear in the ex officio records. 'Instance' causes would be generally initiated at the instance of one of the parties, hence the name.

VISITATIONS. A Visitation was originated by a mandate from the bishop's or archdeacon's official to the clergy and churchwardens of each parish to attend him at a specified time in a specified place. Parishes were, as they still are now, grouped in deaneries and the meetings were arranged for one or two deaneries at a time in one of their churches specified.

These meetings gave the opportunity to require the clergy to produce their letters of orders, certificate of institution or induction, licence to preach or other evidence that might be required. They enabled a check to be made of non-resident clergy and that each parish was duly served by an incumbent or curate. (There were in those days neither official diocesan directories, as there are today, nor any equivalent of 'Crockford'). Further, churchwardens were required to make their 'presentments', which were reports on the ecclesiastical offences or derelictions in their parish. These might include complaints against the clergy as well as the parishioners or be against the patron of a living, who was usually responsible for the structure of the chancel of a church. Churchwardens were sworn in at the annual Visitation, also one or two parishioners as sidemen* or assistants to the churchwardens.

The Visitation also gave opportunity for collection of fees or dues outstanding and there are occasional marginal notes of the amounts of these. It is evident that testamentary matters were raised on occasion, as there are some probate matters dealt with in these records.

The Visitation records are in two parts, the 'libri cleri', sometimes referred to as 'call books', which list the clergy etc. and the 'detecta et comperta',** which record the consequent presentments and the action taken on them. Unfortunately, the action is often left blank, but, on the other hand there is sometimes a very full statement of the proceedings as will be seen on Plate 2. The list in Appendix 1 shows that the series of volumes of the Archdeacon's Court is fairly complete for this period, but for the Commissary's Court the libri cleri are missing except for 'exempt parishes'.***

---

* Sidemen's duties were later confirmed by Canon 90 of 1603.

** There seems to be little difference between the two words used for these ecclesiastical offences. Detecta are, perhaps, rather things found out by searching, whereas comperta are more those lying open - apparent The single word detecta is used here to cover both.
*** See next page.

INTRODUCTION

The 'libri cleri' are not reproduced here, as nothing short of complete transcription would be of any value. They are, however, used for the analysis of the clergy in 1559-61 set out in Appendix 3 and there are occasionally detecta, in the form of marginal or terminal notes, some of which have been used. The immediately preceding libri cleri for 1556, 1557 and 1558 have been published by the Catholic Record Society.*

There are two Archdeacon's Visitations in each of the years being dealt with here. The libri cleri of the Spring Visitation are headed 'Capitulum Generale', or simply 'Generale' (General Chapter). The second Visitation in Autumn or Winter is headed 'Visitacio'. The Visitations of 1559-1562 are all conducted by Stephen Nevinson, the archdeacon's official, and those from 1563 on by Vincent Denne.

EXEMPT PARISHES. Certain parishes were exempt from the jurisdiction of the Archdeacon and are termed 'exempt parishes'.** A Visitation of the exempt parishes was made by the Commissary or his Surrogate, but there is no Elizabethan record of such full Visitation extant till November 1561, though there is that of a General Chapter of April 1560. In both cases the Commissary's Surrogate is the same man as the Archdeacon's Official, Stephen Nevinson.

VISITATION ARTICLES. It has been the general practice in later times for a Visitation to be preceded by the issue from the visiting authority of 'articles of inquiry' to each parish for reply, but these are scarce in these early days. There were Royal Articles at the beginning of each reign at this time*** which, no doubt, formed a basis for inquiries. It happens, however, that the articles for the Archdeacon's Visitation of 1559 have survived**** and the items will be found reflected in the 'detecta'.

At the end of the liber cleri of the General Chapter for 1561 there is a special list of Directions to clergy, presumably as the result of

---

* Vols. 45 and 46 (1950-1). The last was in September 1558, only a few weeks before the death of Queen Mary.

** For information on the exempt parishes see 'Canterbury Administration' by Irene Churchill (S.P.C.K., 1933), vol.1, p.83 and 'Medieval Ecclesiastical Courts in the Diocese of Canterbury' by Brian L. Woodcock (O.U.P., 1952), p.21. For a list of the parishes see 'Wills and Where to Find Them' by J.S.W.Gibson (Phillimore 1974) p.71.

*** 'Visitation Articles and Injunctions' by W.H. Frere, Alcuin Club Collections: 1547, vol.XV, p.103; 1554, vol.XV, p.322; 1559, vol.XVI, p.1.

**** Idem, vol.XVI, p.58. The 'very interesting Visitation Book' and the detecta referred to are presumably the volume Z. 3. 8. included here, as this is the only volume of the date having detecta bound in with the libri cleri. The articles for 1559 appear in full as an appendix to the 'Report of the Lower House of Convocation 1885', no.183, p.64.

inquiries at the Chapter and given as a warning for the main Visitation at the end of that year. These are included in Appendix 4.

ROYAL INJUNCTIONS. Besides the Royal Articles of Inquiry published at the beginning of the reign of Elizabeth I, there was a set of Royal Injunctions to govern the general administration and practice of the Church.* These repeat similar Injunctions of Edward VI in 1547 with amendments and extensions. Brief headings to indicate their nature are set out in Appendix 2. They were required to be read publicly in church once a quarter and complaints will be found of failure to read them accordingly.

PRESENTMENTS. At or before the time of the Visitation the church-wardens were required to produce their 'bill' of presentments. These were usually dealt with by the Archdeacon's official at a separate sitting, but occasionally the note of action appears in the 'liber cleri'.

FORM OF RECORD. The form of a liber cleri record will be seen from the reproduction on Plate 1. The Registrar or his clerk set out beforehand the names of the parishes classified by deaneries, leaving space in which to make entries at the Visitation of the names of the clergy, churchwardens, etc. Some such names as expected were also entered in advance, as there are alterations evidently made at the Visitation, where there had been, perhaps, recent changes. Entries are mainly in Latin.

In the case of detecta records, a similar arrangement of parish headings was made with the presentments entered under each parish. These with the name of the party and a note of the reason for appearnace were generally written in advance, with space left for entry of the action taken - sometimes there was not enough space, sometimes too much. The example on Plate 2 must not be taken as typical, as in some cases no note of action is made, or there is only a formal record of non-appearance, contumacy (the equivalent of contempt of court) and adjournment, or, perhaps, repeated contumacy and excommunication. If there were no presentments, there would be an entry such as 'omnia bene'. These matters would be dealt with at or soon after the Visitation.

There was also kept an 'act book' for what might be called general sittings and detecta entries could appear in this, adjourned from the Visitation sitting. Sittings might be held in various places, even the Judge's house, but the Church of St. Margaret Canterbury seems to have been a favourite one. The formal seat of the Consistory Court was in the Cathedral and that was even used on occasion by the Archdeacon for his court.

In the act books the date and place of each sitting is usually given, but in the Visitation sittings a heading at the beginning of the series is often the only guide.

---

* W.H. Frere, op. cit., vol.XVI, p.8.

INTRODUCTION

SPECIAL NOTES. On occasion there are evidently questions of special importance put to the clergy and churchwardens. In the General Chapter of 1561 there is regular enquiry as to attendance for catechism, and in 1565 paving of the space where altars were removed is frequently mentioned in the detecta. In the Visitation of 1561, including that of the exempt parishes, there is constantly a note that the rood loft has or has not been pulled down. A Visitation of exempt parishes in 1565* shows that churchwardens were then required to return the number of households and number of communicants in their parish and this was regularly done and noted. Unfortunately, the corresponding records for general parishes for that year are wanting.

HANDWRITING. Apart from the sometimes engrossed headings and most of the entries made before the Visitation, the handwriting is often very scribbled, especially in marginal notes evidently hurriedly made. The writer had no thought of writing for posterity but only for making memoranda mainly for his own use.

SPELLING. Spelling is very much phonetic, very different spellings being sometimes found for the same name: Churden or Jurden; Audley or Odleye; Kelie or Caylye and even Segeswick or Sixeweek'. In making extracts surnames are copied exactly as written, but otherwise spelling has been modernised for easy reading. The original wording has, however, been kept as far as possible.

DETECTA. The detecta records set out the offences and faults found by the churchwardens in their presentments and in many cases state the action taken. They cover a great variety of matters, as the analysis of the earliest of Elizabeth's reign extant set out in Appendix 5 shows.

The parson's name is often given the prefix 'Sir'. This is not for a royal knighthood but is probably a courtesy translation of 'dominus', which is found prefixed in the latinized entries in the libri cleri.

When some order is made involving action, a date is often given by which performance is to be certified, usually the next suitable sitting or Visitation.

The principal penalties inflicted were penance, purgation** or excommunication. An entry of excommunication in these records is only of an order for the formal written document to be prepared.*** It may be in some cases that the delinquent returned and was absolved before the excommunication became effective. The excommunication when received was published in the offender's parish church.

---

* Z. 3. 8. ff.132-143.

**For some account of the process of purgation see Burn's 'Ecclesiastical Law' under that title. The entry here usually states the number of 'compurgators' who are to be produced, using a phrase such as 'quarta (manu)' - with a fourth hand - meaning that three others besides himself were required to swear to his innocence. Articles on penance and excommunication will also be found in Burn's volumes.

*** See Appendix 9.

Sometimes a monition to behave in future was given instead of a penalty. Though there was no power to levy fines as such, in some cases a gift to the poor seems to be a condition of discharge. There was no power of imprisonment, though, in the case of a person excommunicate for 40 days or more, application could be made for his arrest to the Court of Chancery by a certificate of the fact from the bishop (referred to as a 'significavit'). That Court would issue a writ 'de excommunicato capiendo' to the sheriff who would have him arrested. He could be imprisoned till he submitted to the ecclesiastical court. By submitting and doing penance for his offence an excommunicate could usually obtain absolution.

ROYAL VISITATION OF 1559. There was a Royal Visitation by Commissioners at the beginning of the Queen's reign. Record of the Visitation of Canterbury Cathedral is extant, but there is apparently no surviving record of this Visitation for the rest of the diocese, except the appointment of the Commissioners.*

METROPOLITICAL VISITATION OF 1560. Apart from the normal Visitations made on behalf of a diocesan bishop, there was occasionally a 'Metropolitical Visitation', when the Archbishop exercised his right of Visitation over the whole Province. A record of such a Visitation of the Canterbury diocese from 19 September to 28 September appears in the Archbishop's register of the time.** There are few 'detecta' in the register entries.

There is a volume of detecta headed 'Reformaciones detectorum in Visitacione Metropolitica' for 1561.*** Dating is very intermittent, but, as it is for the year following the Visitation, it looks like a follow-up volume of uncompleted cases.

Both the above are at Lambeth Palace Library.

SELECTION. There is a large number of entries which state the complaint quite barely, others give fuller particulars. Again, many have no record of the action taken, or such record as is given may be only a brief note of adjournment. Selection has been made of those items which give information likely to be of interest in throwing light on contemporary life. These are not necessarily extensive entries: quite a short one may give the value of a sheep or cow, refer to some local custom or indicate the punishment. In some cases there is a long entry, but, of course, only a précis can be given here.

ARRANGEMENT. Each section is, where practicable, divided by subheadings and in some cases marginal subheadings give guide to detail. There is necessarily overlapping. The same charge may include blasphemy, drunkenness and adultery: it is unnecessary to repeat it as the index of subjects should point to each.

---

* 'Alcuin Club Collections', vol.XVI, p.49; 'The Elizabethan Religious Settlement' by H.N. Birt (1907), p.177.

** 'Parker Register', vol.1, ff.306v-311r; 'Alcuin Club Collections, vol.XVI, p.81.

*** VC 111/4.

INTRODUCTION

REFERENCES. References are given to the original volume and folio number. Dates are not given for each item, as they are often not available, but the list of volumes in Appendix 1 will indicate approximate date.

If reference should be made to the original volume Z. 3. 5., this is a composite volume in which folios have been mixed in binding. Somebody has marked the correct order of folios in green ink and this referencing has been followed here.

There are other composite volumes with folio numbering straight through. In the case of X. 1. 2. however, each part is numbered separately. Reference given thus: 1/43 is to folio 43 of the first part.

In the examples given what precedes the reference is normally the presentment: what follows the reference is the record of action at the hearing, often including subsequent hearings. There are unfortunately many records ending with a note of adjournment, of which there seems to be no further mention. Some entries in the latest volume used (X. 1. 7.) are, no doubt, followed up in a later one.

II

THE CLERGY

Lack of clergy and non-residence are constant cries, often coupled with the complaint of consequent lack of hospitality. There was no hesitation in accusing the clergy of failure in their duty or of misbehaviour.

It should be noted that the term parson is restricted at this time to the rector or patron of the parish and is not used of the vicar or curate. There are cases where the Archbishop or the Dean and Chapter are described as the parson on whom some liability devolves. It was common to 'farm out' the parson's rights and duties. The farmer, who might be a layman, would receive the tithes and other income of the benefice and be responsible for providing someone to serve the cure. One must remember when meeting the word 'farmer' here that it is used in this sense.

1   Chancel needs covering to the value of 20s. Alex Nevill is farmer for my Lord of Canterbury the patron. (Elmsted, X. 1. 7. 124v)

LACK OF CLERGY. The extent of the shortage of clergy at this time can be gauged from the table in Appendix 3. On the other hand, many of the parishes had a very small population and there could not have been really full time work in them. The incumbent did not expect to give his full time and, compared with the standard of today, he must have had an easy life.

It will be seen from the above-mentioned table that readers appear in 1560. The office of reader was formally introduced by Archbishop Parker's 'Order for serving cures now destitute', probably in 1559. Its terms are given in Strype's 'Life and Acts of Archbishop Parker', sections 65 and 66 (pp.131-2) or Strype's 'Annals of the Reformation', vol. 1, sections 185 and 186 (pp.276-7). A summary of the use of readers in the time of Elizabeth I is included in the 'Report to the Convocation of Canterbury, Readers and Sub-deacons', No.383 of 1904, pp.21-27.

2   They have no parson, vicar nor curate. (Chillenden, X. 1. 2. 1/21r)

3   No minister but a reader. (Bonnington X. 1. 5. 52v)

THE CLERGY

NON-RESIDENCE AND PLURALITY. The system of farming the parsonage resulted in many cases of non-residence and the holding of more than one benefice had the same result. The list in Appendix 5 shows the substantial number of such complaints.

4   Church has been vacant for 5 years. The Queen is patron and should provide a curate. Fruits 5 li p.a. 6 li more was given out of the Abbey of Langdon at the suppression, but taken away in Cranmer's time. (W. Langdon X. 1. 5 107v)

5   Cure unserved because George Bingham keeps away the accustomed pension of 4 li p.a. Vicarage has been vacant for 4-5 years. (Guston, Z. 3. 8. 118v)

6   Parson Sir Christopher James is not resident and has other benefices of Folkestone, Dymchurch, New Romney and Hope (St. Mary in the Marsh, X. 1. 3. 35v)

7   Sir Gregory Dodds is Dean of Exeter so is not resident and has left his cure to a deacon who cannot celebrate Communion. (Smarden, X. 1. 2. 1/34v, X. 1. 3. 71v)

8   Parson is a petty canon of Rochester and not resident. (Ulcombe, X. 1. 3. 43v)

9   William Horwood rector is to produce dispensation for non-residence and plurality. (Wormshill, X. 1. 5. 174r)

10 Vicar is non-resident and does not keep hospitality. (Rodmersham, X. 1. 3. 142v)

11 Vicar has Upper Hardres, Stelling, Benenden and Brightling in Sussex. (Lenham, X. 1. 3. 49v)

12 Parson (John Warner) is Dean of Winchester where he lives. No minister. (Harrietsham, X. 1. 3. 41v)

13 Vicar Sir Simon Clarke is parson of Murston and has a preachership in Canterbury. It is not known if he has licence or dispensation. (Milton by Sittingbourne, X. 1. 5. 77v)

14 Robert Carior vicar of Brabourne and rector of Hastingleigh produced letters of institution and dispensation for these benefices granted by Cardinal Pole dated 5 Kalends Decembris 1556. (Z. 3. 5. 188r)

15 Parson comes twice a year for his money and rents, but does not relieve the parish or give anything. (St. Margaret Canterbury, X. 1. 5. 88v)

16 Robert Halman vicar of Leysdown produced letters of 14 May 1561 of dispensation to hold other benefice besides Leysdown. (Z. 3. 7. 23v)

FAILURE IN DUTY. The main categories under this head are failure or irregularity in teaching, preaching or conducting Services, with particular attention to the Queen's Injunctions.

17 Parson does not instruct parishioners how they ought to receive Communion. (Barfreston, X. 1. 2. 1/20r)
18 Catechism is not taught. (Lenham, X. 1. 3. 50v) Curate answers that the youth do not come.
19 Paternoster, Creed and Ten Commandments are not taught. (Preston by Faversham, X. 1. 2. 1/42v)
20 No quarter sermons. (Upper Hardres & Stelling, X. 1. 5. 99v, Lenham X. 1. 3. 49v)
21 No quarter sermons. Very badly served as vicar seldom comes. (Kennington, X. 1. 5. 42v)
22 Sermons not made monthly. (St. Mary in the Marsh, X. 1. 2. 1/56r)
23 No sermons since Michaelmas because of the plague. (Kingsnorth, X. 1. 5. 50v)
24 No sermons the last quarter as the church is burned. Kenardington, X. 1. 5. 56v)
25 Homilies are not read. (Sheldwich, X. 1. 3. 129v)
26 Curate of Worth comes once a month or two months, tolls the bell and before anybody can come he is gone. He leaves half the Service out. We have not had English Litany this half year (Z. 3. 8. 34v, 35r) He denied. The churchwardens to provide a book of prayers and Communion. Curate said that a decree was made in Mr. Collens' time that parishioners of Worth should go to Eastry for Service. (101v) He reads a few homilies and then goes.
27 Queen's Injunctions are not read. (Lenham, X. 1. 3. 49v) They had been read by the clerk not the curate.
28 Vicar admits to Communion some who cannot say the Commandments and Lord's Prayer. (Hoath, Z. 3. 8. 91v). Monished to examine them.
29 Sir Henry Holtbie curate ministered Communion to Agnes Conny without penance or reconciliation. (St. Mary Northgate, Canterbury, X. 1. 5. 92v)
30 Lord's Prayer, Creed and Commandments are not taught every holy day because Service is every second Sunday. (Stalisfield, X. 1. 2. 1/48r)
31 Parson hires out his benefice and distributes nothing. (Ruckinge, X. 1. 2. 1/53r)
32 Vicar will not relieve the poor nor pay what he promised the collectors for this. (Bethersden, X. 1. 4. 72v). Did not appear and was excommunicated.
33 Parson does not distribute 40th part of his fruits according to Queen's Injunctions (Woodchurch, Z. 3. 8. 108v, Whitstable, X. 1. 7. 117v, Hythe, Z. 3. 8. 157v)

THE CLERGY

34 Parson has not preached for 12 months, nor administered the Sacrament this ¼ year. Though warned that an old man wanted Communion, he did not go or send to him. A lame maid prepared herself three times, but he did not come and she died without Communion.(Stelling, X. 1. 3. 96v)

35 John Balkam in danger of death, having no minister, sent for the parson of Otterden who came and promised to minister to him, but failed to do so, and he died without such comfort. (Stalisfield, X. 1. 3. 127v)

36 Robert Browne vicar negligently administered Communion at Easter, allowing the parish clerk to officiate. (Chilham, Y. 2. 24. 129r) He was directed to read to his parishioners next Sunday a written declaration of his fault and negligence in a specified form. Further, at his own expense he was to provide the book of Musculus* in English and study from time to time certain chapters of it for his better understanding and information of his duty.

37 No Services on Wednesdays and Fridays (Broomfield, X. 1. 4. 107v)

38 No Services for ten years. (Stockbury, X. 1. 5. 81v)

39 Vicar refused to obey a mandate through fear of the magistrates. (New Romney, Y. 2. 24. 7r), Penance imposed.

40 Reader does not say his Service in due time. He does not read the Catechism to the youth. (Goodnestone by Faversham, X. 1. 2. 1/49v). He says he does his duty, but the children do not come.

41 All persons of discretion receive Communion; they are not examined in the Catechism. (Lenham, X. 1. 3. 50v, 51r)

42 Thomas Ickham rector married a couple without banns. (St.Andrew, Canterbury, Y. 2. 24. 3r) Penance ordered in church next Sunday, but commuted for payment to the poor box of 5s at Easter in the presence of the churchwardens and six parishioners.

43 Though at his house on May Day and the Sunday before, the vicar refused to come to church for Communion. He sent people home and said he would minister there. (New Romney, Z. 3. 8. 162v)

44 Christopher Warryner of Canterbury, lately anchorite, did not come to Common Prayer at Christ Church twice a week as enjoined by the Queen's Visitors. (Y. 2. 24. 5v). He pleaded infirmity in part, but admitted that he had not been to his own parish church. Directed to go there weekly for Divine Service.

---

* Presumably a work by Wolfgang Musculus translated into English and printed in London in 1563 entitled 'Commonplaces of Christian Religion gathered by W.Musculus for the use of such as desire theKnowledge of Godly Truth' (S.T.C. 18308). There are other publications by Musculus, but this seems the most likely.

45 Richard Pashe married a couple in a prohibited period* without a dispensation. (New Romney, Y. 2. 24. 7r) Penance ordered for both parties and then for Pashe.

46 Henry Baker married a couple in a prohibited period* (Sevington, Y. 2. 24. 20r). He submitted and was absolved.

47 Richard Okeley of Canterbury and Thomas Rawlyns of the Queen's Chapel for celebrating marriage of Johnes and Walker when the parties were excommunicated. (Y. 2. 24. 60r)

48 Nicholas Brett curate for marrying persons without a licence. (St. Mary Magdalen, Canterbury, Y. 2. 24. 45r) To show cause why he should not be suspended from ministration.

49 Richard Dawber a public reader without authority. (Bilsington, Y. 2. 24. 125v) .Warned not to read again. The farmer directed to provide a proper curate before Pentecost.

50 John Holmes reader without authority. (Shadoxhurst, Y. 2. 24. 126r). Warned not to read further.

51 Robert Halman vicar to produce letters of institution and induction. (Leysdown, Y. 2. 24. 34v) Did not appear. Excommunicated.

52 Robert Pyborne, lately curate of Ringwould, licensed to serve any cure and to certify his place of service. (Y. 2. 24. 41v)

53 Andrew Petenden curate of Sutton received 20 nobles and the small tithes of both parishes for serving Guston and Buckland. (Y. 2. 24. 57r). His accounts to be examined.

54 Curate married a couple without Epistle, Gospel or Communion. (St. Mary Magdalen Canterbury, X. 1. 2. 1/6r)

55 Sir Robert Holman has lost the register book. (Ospringe, X. 1. 3. 123v)

56 Sir Edward Perott vicar has not preached against the usurped power of the Pope these twelve months, nor declared against the abuse of images, relics and reported miracles. (Preston by Faversham, X. 1. 2. 1/42v)

57 The vicar does not give warning of Ember Days. (St. Paul Canterbury, X. 1. 3. 4r)

58 Michael Elgor christened a child on a working day. Littlebourne, X. 1. 2. 1/9v, Y. 2. 24. 29v). Monished to appear in the Consistory Court. 28 July 1560. Did not appear. Excommunicated and letters of excommunication affixed to the Cathedral door.

MISBEHAVIOUR There are, perhaps, border line cases between failur in duty and misbehaviour, but cases of gross negligence, drunkenness, gambling and sexual offences would come under the latter head.

---

* A list of fees for dispensation ca.1580 is given in a volume of licence records and is quoted in 'Canterbury Licences (General) 1568-1646' by Arthur J. Willis (1972), p. 115.

THE CLERGY

59 Richard Kirrye for playing at cards and tables. (Ruckinge, X. 8. 5. 67v, X. 1. 2. 53r). Purgation quinta manu.

60 Gilbert Heron vicar for ambulation in church irreverently. (Elmsted, X. 8. 5. 9v) Playing at tables (Y. 2. 24. 82r)

61 Gilbert Heron vicar is an open enemy of God's Word and will not read it. He says the Service darkly, ignorantly and too fast, so that nobody is edified and can pray with him. He is a drinker and player of dice, cards, bowling and other unlawful games. A blind leader of the blind. 'The Lord move you by some means to rid him from us'. (Elmsted, X. 1. 2. 27r-28v X. 8. 5. 57v). Monished to reform himself in all these things.

62 Vicar Richard Dunslake used the company of his wife's daughter very familiarly. (Rolvenden, X. 1. 5. 157r & v)

63 Parson Sir Thomas Langley is married to a woman who was with child in Queen Mary's days and whose husband is thought to be alive. There were no banns, neither was she admitted by two Justices. (Boughton Malherbe, X. 1. 3. 69v)

64 Vicar Sir Robert Holman has made a contract with a woman in the parish whom we suspect he does not intend to marry. In spite of warning, Ellen Wells went to the vicarage, feigned herself sick and lay all night in the vicar's bed while he sat by the fire. (Kennington, X.1.3. 65v, 66r) She appeared. Purgation quarta manu and not to associate with Holman except in public.

65 Curate Sir Charles Askew has two wives, if not three. (Minster Sheppey, X. 1. 4. 131v)

66 John Blackhall curate of Ivychurch comes here and keeps company with a widow three of four days and nights a week. (Shadoxhurst, X. 1. 5. 49v)

67 Parson has cut down trees and taken them to Boughton Blean (Goodnestone by Faversham, X. 1. 5. 73v)

68 Parson sets a very bad example, living 40 miles away from his wife. (St. Mildred Canterbury, X. 1. 5. 92v)

69 John Fuller vicar excommunicate is now reconciled with Thomas Browning gent and is ready to administer Communion to him. (Ashford, X. 1. 6. 9r)

70 Thomas Thompson vicar of Godmersham and Challock for sorcery and incantations (veneficium. cantaciones). (Y. 2. 24. 54r). Excommunication published by vicar of Chilham. Appeared and absolved. To appear in Consistory Court after Michaelmas to answer charges.

71 Richard Kirrey rector of Ruckings for adultery with Margaret Laken. (X. 8. 5. 10v) He denied. Purgation sexta manu for him, quinta for her. He admitted depositions and submitted. Penance in Cathedral and in the church of Ruckings. (11r) 23 April. Penance certified. Further penance ordered in public market place, twice at Ashford and once at Canterbury. To pay 66s. 8d. for charity.

MISCELLANEOUS. There are a number of cases which are, perhaps, best classified under this heading.

72 Service is done very late, not till 12 o'clock, so that parishioners living two miles away cannot get back to Evening Prayer the same day. (Rolvenden, X. 1. 5. 156v & 157r). Directed that Service is to be ended by 11 o'clock.

73 Communion is ministered in fine manchet bread. (Elmstone, X. 1. 5. 103v)

74 Communion is ministered in loaf bread. (Woodnesborough, X. 1. 5. 106v)

75 Communion is not ministered in wafer bread but in fine common bread. (Preston by Wingham, X. 1. 5. 102v)

76 Communion is ministered with popish singing and bread with a print on it. (Broomfield, X. 1. 4. 107v & 108r)

77 Former vicar, Clement Norton, took away Latin books which were for Church Service in Queen Mary's time. (Faversham, X. 1. 2. 1/44v)

78 Thomas Ware clerk said he had not administered Communion in any parish church since the Queen's reign. His portes* is at Mistress Rep's and the old mass book is there too. He subscribed at Sittingbourne at the Visitation. (Z. 3. 7. 37r). He was warned to appear and bring his breviary and mass book and to attend Divine Service in the church of Lynsted on Sundays.

79 Vicar of Brookland says his breviary was burnt in his chamber and the mass book was delivered. (Z. 3. 7. 39v) Purgation quarta manu was ordered.

80 When Communion is administered, it is done in a black gown or such apparel as they do wear. (Sutton by Dover, X. 1. 3. 117v)

81 Vicar Richard Pashe read 'place libera me' at the funeral of Mistress Padjam. (New Romney, Y. 2. 24. 30r)

82 Vicar John Fuller brought a corpse to church in surplices. (Ashford, Y. 2. 24. 86v)

83 Sir Robert Thompson parson has pulled down part of the house to botch up the rest. He has sold timber that was about the grounds. (Goodnestone by Faversham, X. 1. 3. 124v)

84 John Barton forbad Mr. Clarke parson of Murston to say the Service at Sittingbourne, so depriving all. (Sittingbourne, X. 1. 4. 122v) Barton said he proved Mr. Clarke a very dissembler at (? as) ever did eat bread.

---

*i.e. 'portuis' referred to in Appendix 7 (page 76)

THE CLERGY

85 Parson should find a clerk, as has been the custom. Now there is none. (Staplehurst, X. 1. 3. 52v)

86 Mr. Russell in his sermon called the churchwardens 'false procured dogs'. (Gt Chart, X. 1. 3. 65v)

87 Parson does not exhort parishioners to be warned of the threatenings of God. (Hastingleigh, X. 1. 3. 91v)

88 Parson does not instruct us to avoid superstition. He does not teach that health and grace come from God. (Boughton Malherbe, X. 1. 3. 68v)

89 Vicar lacks a square cap. (Doddington, X. 1. 5. 74v)

90 Parson does not wear a cornered cap as others do. (St. Mildred, Canterbury, X. 1. 5. 92v)

III

CHURCH BUILDINGS AND PRECINCTS

The maintenance of the chancel of a church was normally the responsibility of the parson, the rector or patron of the benefice. Repair of the body of the church, churchyard, etc. was the liability of the parish and a 'sess' (assessment or rate) was made from time to time to levy the cost from parishioners.

There are very many entries of need to repair with little or no detail. Those given here are selected for the information they give.

91 Chancel needs repair, fault of the Archdeacon of Canterbury. (Doddington, X. 1. 4. 117v)

92 A chancel window in decay, both stone and glass. Fault of the Dean & Chapter of Rochester. (Sutton Valence, X. 1. 4. 100v)

93 Chancel unrepaired, Mr. Lovelace believed bound. Benefice was impropriated to the late dissolved monastery of St. Gregory near Canterbury. (Bekesbourne, X. 1. 5. 98v)

94 Chancel much in decay. Defiled with doves. (Halstow, X. 1. 2. 1/43v, X. 1. 4. 128v)

95 Chancel much in decay. My Lord of Canterbury should repair it. (Erabourne, X. 1. 4. 56v)

96 My Lord of Canterbury's Grace is in default for the chancel. (Marden, X. 1. 3. 45v)

97 Some lead taken away at the chancel door letting rain in. Chancel pavement is broken and uncleanly where Communion is received. (Biddenden, X. 1. 5. 45v)

98 Church needs repair, especially glass windows shaken by thunder. (Stone, X. 1. 7. 52v)

99 Church needs shingling, tiling and glazing, charges will come to 13 li 6s 8d. (Sheldwich, X. 1. 7. 149v). Churchwardens to make a cess or tax of 5 li, half to be collected by Lady Day next and the other half by 1 May and to be spent on repairs done by Lammas Day.

100 Church and steeple need repair to value of 6 li 13s 4d. (Sturry, X. 1. 7. 66v)

CHURCH BUILDINGS AND PRECINCTS

101 The body of the church needs repair and the steeple is in decay. (Shepherdswell, X. 1. 7. 172v, 173r) The churchwardens are to make a sess or tax of 5 marks, one half to be collected by the (feast of the Annunciation) and the other half by Midsummer Day. Repairs are to be done by Michaelmas and certified at the Visitation.

102 Church and chancel are in decay for that the lead of the church was stolen. The charges of the church and the amending thereof will cost 40s. The charges of the chancel will cost 6 li, for that the windows lack glazing, so that neither curate nor communicants are able to sit about the table for the vehemence of the wind and for the filth of doves and owls. (Sandhurst, X. 1. 7. 15v, X. 1. 3. 59v)

103 The church of Warden is ruined ('corruit'). (Z. 3. 5. 148v). Marginal note: 'accedant ad alias ecclesias'.

104 There is no separation between church and chancel as it was burned by misfortune. (Lynsted. X. 1. 5. 69v)

105 Parsonage house is decayed and has been unusable for a dozen years. Bishop of Canterbury is owner and Arnold Dunkyn the farmer. (Elmsted, X. 1. 4. 52v)

106 Parsonage barn was pulled down by the late parson and sold for 40s. (St. Mary in the Marsh, X. 1. 4. 65v)

107 Vicarage needs repair, both tiling and walls, also the pigeon house, will cost 4 li. (Newington by Hythe, X. 1. 7. 136v)

108 Parsonage house, called the Hospital of Poor Priests, is part fallen down and the rest ready to fall. (St. Margaret, Canterbury, X. 1. 5. 88v)

109 Bakehouse and kitchen and other chambers of the parsonage are in great decay, to the value of 5 li. (Sandhurst, X. 1. 7 16v)

110 Vicarage is in ruin and churchyard filthy. Vicar lives in an alehouse. (Benenden, X. 1. 5. 159v)

111 Parishioners will not meet to make an assessment for repair of church and churchyard much in decay. (Linton, X. 1. 5. 63v). Letters directing a cess are to be sent to the churchwardens.

112 Churchyard is very noisomely kept and uncleanly. (Hythe, Z. 3. 8. 44v)

113 Churchyard is unenclosed. (Harrietsham, X. 1. 3. 41v)

114 Churchyard not well fenced, nor decently kept. (Newnham, X. 1. 5. 71v) Plomer directed to gather the parishioners to make a cess.

115 Churchyard not sufficiently fenced. Dispute with Mr Ager where it should go. (Otterden, X. 1. 5. 74v)

116 Parish keeps enclosure of churchyard and vicar fells the timber. (Postling, X. 1. 5. 124v)

IV
CHURCH FITTINGS AND FURNISHINGS

In the record of the Visitation of exempt parishes in November 1561 there is general notice given that rood lofts are to be pulled down promptly (Z. 3. 8. 14v, 17r), pulpits are to be provided before Candlemas next in all places where they are not convenient under penalty of 10s (Z. 3. 8. 21v) and books of homilies for Palm Sunday and homilies for gange* week are to be provided (Z. 3. 8. 17r).

That special attention was given to the removal of rood lofts is emphasised by marginal notes against the entries of many parishes in the libri cleri of that year (Z. 3. 7., and for exempt parishes Z. 3. 8.), certifying that the rood loft is down.

There are many entries that the parish lacks the Paraphrase**. This is an English translation of the New Testament, interspersed with a commentary. By the Royal Injunctions of Edward VI of 1547 (No. 7) it was to be provided and set up in every church to be available for parishioners to read. The order was repeated in the Injunctions of Elizabeth (No. 6).

117 Rood loft is standing. All other monuments are destroyed. (Chartham, X. 1. 2. 1/10v)

118 Rood loft is standing and there is a painted table where the high altar stood. (Sandhurst, X. 1. 2 1/29r)

119 No Communion table: it was broken by Mr. Burden of Dover. (Sutton by Dover, X. 1. 3. 117v)

120 The tabernacle is standing. (Ulcombe, X. 1. 3. 42v,43r). Ordered to reform everything before the next General Chapter.

121 Vicar has no key to the poor men's box. (St. Paul, Canterbury, X. 1. 4. 6v)

122 No good surplice for priest or clerk. (Crundale, X. 1. 4. 25v)

---
*Rogation days. This is identified in Visitation Articles and Injunctions by W. H. Frere vol. 3 (Alcuin Club Collections, vol VI), p. 160 as referring to No. 17 in the Second Book of Homilies.

** 'The Paraphrase of Erasmus upon the Newe Testamente': 2 vols. 1548-9.

CHURCH FITTINGS AND FURNISHINGS

123 No poor box or pulpit. (Betteshanger, X. 1. 4. 37v)

124 Chest is broken up and register stolen. (Ashford, X. 1. 4. 70v)

125 No convenient reading desk (Wingham, Z. 3. 8. 96v). Churchwardens agreed to provide desk and pulpit.

126 There are certain monuments of idolatry undefaced on the church walls. (Leeds, X. 1. 4. 98v) Richard Phillipps churchwarden appeared and certified it was defaced and all other things were provided.

127 Glass windows in chancel, chapel and church are undefaced, also stone footstools on which idols stood. Also undefaced are the place where the priest sat on festival days and the hole where the sepulchre was wont to lie. The place where the cruets stood to wash his (the priest's) hands is standing. Doors and steps to rood loft are unmade, holy water stock (? = stoup) is undefaced. Chancel steps are standing. (Bearsted X. 1. 4. 103v). Churchwardens are to see that all is reformed by All Saints Day.

BIBLES AND OTHER BOOKS. (in some cases including other items).

128 Perfect Bibles are lacking at Hardres and Stelling as they are without the New Testament. Surplices are evil and (imperfect), no Communion book, but so it was in King Edward's time. (Upper Hardres, Z. 3. 7. 49v)

129 Bible is incomplete, chapters torn out and not of the largest size. Also lacking a surplice, book of common Services, Paraphrase, homilies, Communion table, cloth and cup, seat for minister and chest for register. (Buckland by Faversham X. 1. 5. 68v). Direction given to Thomas Furmynger to provide by Michaelmas.

130 Sir John Burnell vicar of Alkham, the last minister here, had chalice, books and other church ornaments. (Charlton, X. 1. 4. 49v)

131 Lack a Bible of the greatest volume also the Paraphrase of Erasmus on the Gospels, because the vicar is not ready to pay his part. (Preston by Faversham, X. 1. 2. 1/43r)

132 No Paraphrase. Goodwife Stoddard is farmer of the parsonage and should give half to buy one. (Shepherdswell, X. 1. 7. 173v)

133 Paraphrase and psalter lacking, charges would come to 20s. Would buy if we had parson's money. (River, X. 1. 7. 126v)

134 Paraphrase lacking. My Lord of Canterbury should pay half, but for lack of that money we have not the book as yet. (Brabourne, X. 1. 2. 1/25v)

135 Church Bible was handed to John Wotton for the Commissary, Mr. Collens. (Seasalter, X. 8. 5. 56v, 58r)

CHURCH LIFE IN KENT

136 No Paraphrase for lack of the parson's portion towards buying it. The vicar, Sir John Abbey, after receiving it from Mr. Parkhurste the farmer preached openly that churchwardens and sidesmen were perjured for lack of the Paraphrase. (Stalisfield, X. 1. 4. 117v)

137 Communion book, book of homilies and psalter have been delivered to Mr. Collens to be burnt. (Coldred, X. 1. 2. 1/20v)

138 Homilies for gange days lacking also the little book of prayers set forth by the Archbishop* (St. John Thanet, X. 1. 4. 17v). 5 May. Certified by Mr. Lynch that the book is provided.

139 Bible with other books in Queen Mary's time was delivered to Mr. Henry Bingham but not returned. (Bekesbourne, X. 1. 5. 98v)

140 They have not the last homilies commanded in his Grace's last Visitation. (Brook, X. 1. 5. 103v)

141 Communion book and Bible (were given) to Mr. Harpsfelde Archdeacon of Canterbury.** (Postling X. 1. 2. 1/22r)

142 The Bible is blotted and raced (Ashford, X. 1. 5. 36r). 28 April 1564. Directed to provide a Bible by St. John's Day.

CHALICE AND COMMUNION CUP

There is occasional reference to the parish being without a Communion cup. In 1564 and 1565 there is a number of mentions of converting a chalice into a Communion cup.***

143 No chalice or Communion cup, but have to borrow one. (Betteshanger, X. 1. 4. 37v)

144 Churchwardens are to provide a decent Communion cup by St. Thomas Day. (St. Dunstan, Canterbury, X. 1. 6. 80r)

145 They have no chalice or Communion cup, only a glass. (Preston by Faversham, X. 1. 4. 28v)

146 Ditto. only one of tin. (Hope, X. 1. 4. 67v)

147 Ditto. only one of maple. (Brabourne, X. 1. 4. 56v)

---

*There are a number of references to this little book of prayers being missing. In one case (Kenardington, X. 1. 4. 68v) it is described as 'little book of prayers for dearth, pestilence and the like'. This description may be in error. If so, reference may be to 'Certen godly prayers to be used for sundry purposes' appended to the Prayer Book of 1560.

**Archdeacon in Queen Mary's time.

***The change was from the medieval shape with an open, almost hemispherical, bowl to a cup shape. See 'English Church Plate 597-1830' by Charles Oman (1957), pp. 133-144 and plates 49-72.

CHURCH FITTINGS AND FURNISHINGS

148 In time of the popish mass the vicar, to reverence that order, used to minister in a chalice of silver, whereas now in contempt of this ministration he uses a bowl too unseemly to put milk in or some other homely office. (Elmsted, X. 1. 2. 1/28r)

149 Have no Communion cup, but a chalice which we will alter into a cup. (River, X. 1. 7. 127v)

150 Chalice delivered to Yngram Joll, one of the heads of the parish, to alter into a minister cup of the same weight.(Capel, X. 1. 7. 132v)

151 Churchwardens are to convert the chalice into a decent Communion cup. (Alkham, X. 1. 6. 76r)

152 Ditto. (Womenswold, X. 1. 6. 78r)

153 Churchwarden is to redeem their chalice pledged to Thomas Straugham for 20s, making an assessment for the redemption and buying a Communion cup. (Eastling X. 1. 6. 74r)

154 To make a levy of 4 li (40s scored through) by farming out a cow and buy a decent Communion cup (Lydden X. 1. 6. 76v)

155 (Memo) St. Dunstan, Canterbury. There is in the hands of Mr. Corthopp silver double gilt (29½ oz.) valued at 5s oz. He will supply a cup at 5s oz. ready made by Easter. 'We can give none' (X. 1. 7. 74v)

Amongst miscellaneous papers there is one, which, though of a later date, gives some detail of one of these changes from chalice to Communion cup at Elham, a change evidently still being required over 150 years later (Diocese Miscellaneous, box 5, No. 7).

A Communion cup weighing 13 oz 9 dwt @ 7s oz	4.14. 0
A salver weighing 9oz 8 dwt @ 6s 10d oz	3. 4. 0
Graving of salver and cup	1. 6
	£7.19. 6
Received an old cup	2. 7. 0
	£5.12. 6

Received 20 March 1724/5 the old chalice value 47s.

V
LAYMEN AND THE CHURCH

RECEIVING COMMUNION There are very many entries that an individual does not receive Communion, sometimes within a period stated, sometimes specifically referring to Easter. In normal cases, where the person accused appears, he is monished to receive and the case is dismissed, often only after the receiving has been certified. If he does not appear, he is declared contumacious and, evidently according to the circumstances, the Judge either decrees that letters of excommunication are to issue or he gives a second opportunity for appearance before so acting.

The records of subsequent hearings with their dates are often appended to the record of the first hearing, but there is not always a final decision shown.

Many cases of such formal proceedings do not appear here, those selected being to give additional information or reveal special circumstances.

156 Joan Pickering has not received. (Selling, X. 1. 2. 1/45v) She admitted it and received on Palm Sunday last.

157 John Sympson and wife have not received. (Ashford, X. 1. 6. 3v) Did not appear. Excommunicated.

158 John Howlyn had not received. (Hythe, Z. 3. 8. 157v, 158r) Did not appear. Excommunicated.

159 John Gorham and wife have not received. (Boughton Malherbe, X. 1. 6. 48r, 61r). Undertook to receive next Sunday. Apparitor certified.

160 John Ayer has not received. (New Romney, Z. 3. 8. 160v, 161r) Certified that he had received. Monished to receive more diligently and more often in future.

161 Thomas Harynden and eight others of East Sutton did not receive (X. 8. 5. 75r). One answered that he received after Easter, others that they received at Sutton Valence. They are all to bring certificates.

162 Henry Fowler and seven others absented themselves from church and did not receive. (Holy Cross, Canterbury, X. 1. 4. 4v, 5r) One is ordered to agree with the Churchwardens. Another said he had received at St. Dunstan. Another said he worked at Chartham and went to church there. All are to produce certificates from the churchwardens.

LAYMEN AND THE CHURCH

At Easter

163 Elizabeth Feld widow has not received since a year last Easter. (Boxley, X. 1. 7. 27v, 28r) Certified that she had received.

164 Thomas Grove and wife did not receive at Easter. (Petham, X. 8. 2. 48v, 49r). Certified by the curate that they had received at Ickham.

165 John Allen did not receive at Easter because of divers business of his masters. (Petham, X. 8. 2. 48v, 49r). Said he had already received. Subject to certificate by the curate, dismissed.

166 George Amys did not receive at Easter. (Kennington, X. 1. 6. 82r, X. 1. 7. 5v, 6r) Certified that he had.

167 John Smythe & wife Lettyce have not received since Easter. (Snargate, X. 1. 5. 51v, 52r). Did not appear. Excommunicated. 5 May. He appeared & was absolved. A commission was issued to the curate to absolve her. Both monished to receive in their parish church.

168 Richard Horlocke did not receive at Easter or since, although often warned to do so. (E. Sutton, X. 1. 7. 28v, 29r). He admits he was twice spoken to by the minister and once by the churchwardens. He would have but for Rolf Goorn's wife who forbad him. Again when he had prepared himself the minister was absent. He undertook to receive and receiving was certified. Marginal note: 10d.

169 James Welles has not received since Easter, but has promised to do so. (Wingham, X. 8. 2. 50v, 51r). Certified by the curate that he has received since the bill of presentments.

170 Roger Deale has not received at Easter or since. (Nonington, X. 8. 2. 52v, 53r). He has left the parish.

171 Joan Chambers widow did not receive at Easter. (Deal, X. 8. 2. 58v, 59r). Adjourned till purgation for witchcraft. 5 December. Did not appear. Excommunicated.

Long periods

172 John Taylor has not received for a twelvemonth. (Eastwell, X. 1. 6. 71v, X. 1. 7. 9v, 10r) Certified in prison.

173 James Hynxwell & wife have not received for four years. (Headcorn, Y. 2. 24 113r). Archbishop's Visitation 1563.

174 Christopher Kelsham and eight others have not received since a year last Easter. (Headcorn, Y. 2. 24 113r & v, 114r) Archbishop's Visitation 1563.

175 Francis Weldy she has not received this twelvemonth. (Linton, X. 1. 5. 62v, 63r, X. 1. 7 39v, 40r). Monished to receive with two others at Linton in one of the coming Pentecost feast days. It being alleged that he did not come because he was in debt, he said he had been in London two or three times this twelvemonth. Monished to receive within the next month and to be certified. Gives a bond in 10 li.

176 William Gadder did not receive last year. (Woodnesborough, X. 1. 5. 107v, 108r). Monished to receive in the next three weeks to be certified. Curate of Goodnestone confirmed receiving.

177 Robert Barley had not received this twelvemonth. (Preston by Wingham, X. 1. 5. 102v, 103r). Certified he was ill. Monished to receive with two others next Sunday or the Sunday following in his parish church to be certified. Marginal note: he paid 10d.

178 John Balden has not received for two years. (Hartlip, X. 1. 5. 79v, 80r). He agreed he had not received since a year last Easter. Monished to receive on Sunday and to confess his offence publicly in the form handed to him in writing.

179 Stephen Mathue is very slack in coming to church and has not received for two years. Millicent his wife has not received since Christmas. (St. Mildred, Canterbury, X. 1. 5. 92v, 93r) He went to Newhaven 'in warefare' about two years ago next Michaelmas, where he received, and came home next Easter. Last Easter he received at St. Mildred. Monished to receive in his parish church.

Removed from parish

180 John Arrowsmythe and Elizabeth Hole did not receive last year and now live at Ash. (Woodnesborough, X. 1. 5. 107v, 108r). John monished to receive with his wife in his parish church next Sunday to be certified. 5 May & 12 May. Did not appear. Excommunicated.

With household

181 (blank) Sinckler and widow Goodyn and their households did not receive at Easter. (Northbourne, X. 1. 5. 109v, 110r) He was certified to be in the North. She was cited but did not appear. Adjourned.

Unreconciled, etc.

182 John Collards and three others for receiving Communion when out of charity and unreconciled. (Barham X. 1. 3 110v)

183 George Launder als Fletcher had not received. (Tenterden, X. 1. 5. 154r, 155r & v) He confessed he was not in love and charity with one of the parish. Monished to reconcile himself and receive. Later: curate certified that he received at Christmas.

LAYMEN AND THE CHURCH

184 Agnes Davye did not receive at Easter. (Tenterden, X. 1. 6. 57v) She said she was not in peace with one Hodges of Tenterden who had witheld a legacy. Monished to be reconciled and receive before the Visitation on 9 October.

185 Matilda (Moultt) Bushe did not receive in her parish church. (Harbledown, X. 1. 7. 78v, 79r). She was not in quiet with one of the parishioners. Monished to receive.

186 John Baker did not receive at Easter or since. (Chilham, X. 1. 7. 92v, 93r). There was controversy between him, his wife and William Harryett. Monished to receive before the Feast of the Purification.

187 George Foord has been absent from Communion on pretence of a suit between him and James Baker. (Northbourne, X. 1. 7. 178v, 179r). He is out of patience with Baker. Monished to confer and talk with some learned man in the Word of God to conform and settle his conscience.

188 Davie Mershe has not received for a year. (E Langdon, X. 1. 7. 179v, 180r). He was at variance with Harry Marshe. They both appeared and shook hands in Court and were reconciled. They were monished to receive.

189 William son of Richard Goteley received at Easter without being reconciled. (Throwley X. 1. 4. 114, 115r). He is to admit his fault before the Churchwardens ('habet ad publicandum coram iconomis') to be certified.

ATTENDANCE AT CHURCH There were directions in the Queen's Injunctions about attendance at church, disturbance of preachers and giving quiet attention to the Service*

190 William Wyncke and others do not come to their parish church. (Holy Cross Canterbury, X. 1. 5. 88v, 89r). Did not appear. Excommunicated.

191 Bartholomew Mungen and others do not frequent and use the church as they should. (St. Paul, Canterbury, X. 1. 5. 89v, 90r). Did not appear. Excommunicated.

192 Robert Johnson seldom comes to church to hear Divine Service (Reculver, Z. 3. 8. 88v, 89r). Did not appear. Excommunicated. Later appeared and was absolved. He is to agree with the churchwardens and they are to certify. (X. 8. 2. 55v, 56r). He said he went to Chislet, being in the service of Mr. Consant. To be certified that he was a servant of William Consant. Dismissed.

193 Ralph Rychard came to church though excommunicated and defied the Commissary. (Upchurch, X. 1. 7, 147v, 148r). He is to show cause why the Queen should not be petitioned for his arrest.

---
*Nos. 33, 36, 38 and 46.

194 George Grene is negligent in coming to church. (Eastwell, X. 1. 7. 10v, 11r). Tylly (the apparitor) is given a mandate to certify the truth of the objection.* He certified that Grene attends church.

195 Thomas Packham & his wife absent themselves from church. (Wychling, X. 1. 5. 79v, 80r). He says he was absent only one Sunday.

Poor men

196 Thomas Gyll and others absent themselves from church (St. Paul Canterbury, X. 1. 4. 6v, 7r). The vicar says they are poor and seek their living abroad.

Prison

197 John Dashe is absent from church. (Benenden, X. 1. 5. 45v, 46r). He is in prison in Maidstone.

Dead

198 Roger Swetman has been absent from church for six Sundays. (Deal, Z. 3. 8. 102v, 103r). He is dead.

Age

199 Widow Turk is negligent in coming to church. (Marden, X. 1. 7. 34v, 35r). The vicar certified she is very old.

Infirmity

200 Joan Cobb wife of Thomas Cobb does not come to church. (Reculver, Z. 3. 8. 88v, 89r). Judge monished her to produce a certificate of her infirmity and to agree with the churchwardens. Her husband appeared and satisfied the Judge.

Repeated presentment with detail of penance

201 Thomas Cogger is presented once again for not coming to church. (Stone, X. 1. 7. 54v, 54r) 7 January 1565. He said he was away from home when previously presented but admits he has been negligent in coming to church. He was ordered to do penance by standing before the curate while he was reading the homily with his face towards the people having only a white rod in his hand, and to read a schedule (which will be given him) of the cause of his doing penance. 24 January. He is to give a bond in 10 marks.

Left the parish

202 Henry Peren does not come to church on Sundays and holy days. (Charing, X. 8. 2. 72v, 73r). He has gone away ('aufugit')

---

*i.e. the accusation.

LAYMEN AND THE CHURCH

Attending other church,

203 John Nicholas of Orlestone, monished to keep to his parish church, came to Warehorne, contrary to the Queen's Injunctions. (X. 1. 3. 27v, 28r). He said he went to Warehorne because he was warned by the parson there.

204 John Francklyshe and his wife do not come to their parish church but go to other churches. (Bonnington, X. 1. 3. 36v, 37r). He said they have no Service.

205 John Norden and others do not come diligently to church on the Sabbath. (St. Andrew Canterbury, X. 1. 4. 1v, 2r). One says he goes to St. Mary's or Christ Church. They are monished to be diligent in going to church.

206 (blank) Roydon and others on Sunday 26 March, in contempt of their own church, attended Service at Chartham. (Chilham, X. 1. 5. 104v)

207 Alexander Grigesbye does not go to his own parish church on Sundays, but goes to Linton. (Loose, X. 8. 2. 74v, 75r). He admitted it and was monished to go to his parish church of Loose henceforth under pain of the penalty provided by the statute.* Dismissed. Marginal note: '2s 4d'.

Church distant

208 Davye Dodd his wife & household do not come to church more than five or six times a year. (Chislet, X. 1. 4. 16v, 17r). He says they go to church at Reculver, but often, as the weather serves, he goes to Chislet two long miles away and the ways in the winter very foul. The pew where they sat is now converted to the place for Communion, so 'he shall have election of another'.

209 John Grendell has not been to church five or six times since Easter. (Ivychurch, Z. 3. 8. 109v, 110r). He is four miles from the parish (church) and goes to Brookland.

Working out of the parish

210 Thomas Turner is negligent in coming to church on the Sabbath. (Whitstable, X. 1. 7. 117v, 118r). He said he did not work in the parish. Monished to attend his parish church.

211 John Belvilo has not attended his parish church since Whitsuntide. (Ruckinge, X. 1. 7. 47v, 48r). He was sworn to be at his parish church once a month, if in health and may do so lawfully, otherwise to attend the church where he works.

---

*1 Eliz I, c.2 (See Appendix 7, page 79)

Baptism outside own parish

212   (blank) Robynson caused his child to be christened at Ashford. (Gt. Chart, X. 1. 2. 1/35r)

213   Edward Horden caused his child to be christened out of the diocese and would not suffer his wife to be purified by the minister. (Goudhurst, X.1.2. 1/62v). The child was christened by the midwife at home as it was in jeopardy of death. His wife was purified at home by the priest of Woodhurst, being sick for 10 weeks.

Responsibility for apprentice

214   The two apprentices of Robert Pylling are slack in coming to church. (St. Mary Bredman, Canterbury, X. 1. 7. 76v, 77r) Pylling said he kept the boys at home on Easter Day attending to his horse. They received Communion before All Hallows Day last. He is to give 3s 4d to the poor box tomorrow or next Sunday.

Responsibility for household

215   Martin Cage's wife seldom comes to church. (Westbere, X. 1. 5. 114v, 115r). He appeared and was monished that his wife shall be at Morning Prayer in his own parish church on Whitsunday and the rest of the holy days and Trinity Sunday. This is to be certified at the next (sitting).

216   Symon Helye has four in his house who do not come on Sundays and Holy Days to learn the Catechism. (Eythorne & Waldershare, X. 1. 3. 113v)

217   George Mylles, his wife & servants and John Malyn do not come to church. (St. Mary Bredin, Canterbury, X. 1. 4. 5v, 6r) Mylles' wife is dying. He is monished to go to church with his household. Malyn is to be sought in Thanet where he works.

Prescribed forfeiture*

218   William Wygmore and his household had only been to church once between September and Christmas. He refused to pay the forfeiture under the Act and used railing words. (Warehorne, X. 8. 5. 65v) He said he lived two miles from the church and was at one church or another on Sundays and holy days. To be certified. Certificate was received and the Judge monished him.

219. (blank) Stynton of Betnamswood and others do not come to church and will not pay their forfeiture. (Biddenden, X. 1. 4. 85v, 86r). Stynton was monished to be diligent in attendance, the others to agree with the churchwardens and have their attendance certified. For one purgation septima manu.

220   Some of the parish come very slowly to church and fine is not levied. (Hackington, X. 1. 5. 94v)

---

*1 Eliz c.2. (See Appendix 7, page 79)

LAYMEN AND THE CHURCH

Overseers to supervise attendance

221 John Hudson and John Sacry, appointed overseers to see people come to church* only came twice a quarter themselves. (Headcorn, X. 1. 4. 88v, 89r). Sacry is to show cause why he should not be excommunicated for his negligence. It is certified that he has satisfied (the churchwardens in his duty). Hudson said he was not absent except for the fair.

Miscellaneous

222 Robert Colwell and others were diligent choir in Queen Mary's time, but now will not come. (Faversham, X. 1. 3. 155v).

223 Mrs. Margaret Ellis is absent from church because her husband is buried in the church where her sitting is. She goes to Ashford church. (Kennington, X. 1. 5. 42v, 43r). Did not appear. Excommunicated.

224 Joan daughter of John Howes has not come to church for 10 years. (Sturry, X. 1. 4. 10v, 11r). 'She is a very idyote'.

225 Robert Hixe does not keep his parish church, being a minstrel and a poor man. (Ruckinge, X. 1. 7. 47v, 48r). He agreed to be at his parish church every second Sunday, unless he has lawful excuse.

DUTY OF CHURCH OFFICERS

226 John Mylner, former churchwarden, sold a front cloth, a Lent cloth and a lantern about Michaelmas last and has given no account. (Stone, X. 1. 2. 1/55r)

227 John Mylles and Thomas German sold certain church goods to John Brakinburge for 10s 8d. They have not given in their account as churchwardens. (Wye, X. 1. 2. 1/64v). They appeared and it is to be certified.

228 Robert Aynstone churchwarden and George Waghorne lately sexton gave away a cope, a chasuble, two tunics and three albs to John Rade of this parish who will not restore them or pay. The cope was given by Lawrence Patynden now deceased. (Benenden, X. 1. 2. 1/34r) Aynstone appeared, was absolved and dismissed. The churchwarden is to prosecute in due form of law.

229 George Waghorne whilst sexton took about 20 li from the church without consent. (Benenden, X. 1. 3. 60v, 61r) Vincent churchwarden is to plead the debt in due form of law.

230 John Franklin is to account for sequestration given to him by the Queen's Visitors and he holds 20s given by Nicholas Bisshope for church repairs. (X. 8. 5. 74v). He is to produce certificate. Marginal note: Certified that it is fully accounted for. (Parish not stated).

*Queen's Injunctions No. 46

CHURCH LIFE IN KENT

231 (blank) Colwell and (blank) Belke are very negligent in seeing to good order for coming to church*. Being required to call in the people when Mr. Rydley preached, they suffered the people to dance at the market cross and neglected the sermon. (X. 8. 5. 104r)

232 Henry Questonburye churchwarden has made no account for ten years. (St. Mary Bredman Canterbury, X. 1. 4. 2v, 3r) Monished to produce accounts before St. John Baptist's Day. (X. 1. 7. 76v,77r). Renewed charge. Did not appear. Penalty reserved.

233 Richard Smythson, former parish clerk, took some boards for his own use, value 6s. 8d. (Lower Hardres, X. 1. 5. 95v) Marginal note: He lives at Bridge.

MISBEHAVIOUR IN CHURCH OR PRECINCTS

234 Robert Homes does not come to church. He hurled a pot and drew his dagger at one of the sidemen who spoke to him of it. (Holy Cross Canterbury, X. 1. 3. 9v, 10r). He admits it. Adjourned.

235 Sir David Robson on Easter Day disturbed the minister at Communion and Baptism. (St. Mary Northgate Canterbury, X. 1. 5. 91v, 92r). Monished to be examined on the objection at the Judge's house.

236 (blank) Royton disquieted the vicar (at Chartham) in time of Service. (Chilham, X. 1. 5. 104v)

237 George Brysto talked in church in time of Service and played with a dog while the curate was reading the Paraphrase. (X. 1. 3. 156v)

238 (blank) Barham gent and Edward Marleton. Bloodshed in church. (Barham, X. 1. 7. 107v)

239 William Blacke went out of church during reading of the Epistle. He said he could not abide the doctrine and thought his heart would have burst. (Warehorne, X. 1. 3. 28v, 29r)

240 The wife of Alexander Dence is a talker in church. (Cranbrook, X. 1. 3. 74v)

241 Tomsyn wife of Walter Brykenden is a scold and brawler with Thomas Bowcher in the churchyard during the time of Communion, disturbing the Service. (Rolvenden, X. 1. 2. 1/32v)

SABBATH BREAKING

242 Roger Wycks card playing at his house in time of Divine Service. (Orlestone, X. 1. 7. 51v, 52r)

243 Lyn Tailor a common haunter of alehouses in time of Divine Service. (Chislet, X.8. 5. 61v) Contumacious. Before the Archbishop

---

*Parish not stated. There was a Colwell at Faversham (222 above) also a reader at Preston by Faversham and Belke churchwarden of Sheldwich.

LAYMEN AND THE CHURCH

244 John Godfrey and others being victuallers open their doors and drink in Service time. Thomas Church, being a minstrel, played to dancers in Service time. (Milton by Sittingbourne, X. 1. 5. 83r).

245 Thomas Broke and others being millers grind on Sundays. (parish not stated)(X. 8. 5. 80r). Monished not to grind on Sundays unless necessary by licence of the Judge.

246 John Kevill victualling and playing and Thomas Cutt bowling in time of Divine Service. (St. Mary Northgate, Canterbury, X. 1. 2. 1/2v). They each pay 12d for the poor.

247 Thomas, John and Richard Geffry reaped wheat on Sunday in harvest and did not come to Service. (Stalisfield, X. 1. 3. 127v, 128r). Monished to reconcile themselves with the parishioners and to desist.

248 John Oliver for carrying on Sunday (presumably he was a carrier by trade). (Eastchurch, X. 1. 7. 147v).

POPERY AND DISAFFECTION WITH THE REFORMED SERVICES

The cases entered here are those relating to the individual layman as distinct from the offences of clergy or the retaining of illegal monuments or furnishings of the church, which will be found referred to in previous sections.

249 Margery Inwood wears her beads. (St. Margaret Canterbury, X. 1. 3. 18v, 20v).

250 Randall Tatnall keeps a mass book and other Latin books. (St. Andrew, Canterbury, X. 1. 4. 2v).

251 Widow Maisters has a mass book and an image under her bed head. (Willesborough, Y. 2. 24 94v).

252 Mother Wells derided the present religion and said she hoped they would have mass again shortly. (St. Mary Northgate, Canterbury, X. 1. 5. 91v) Purgation tertia manu.

253 An Irish priest 'straughte of his wyttes' has become a reader of fortunes who gives people charms to defend them from evil and tries to get them to condemn and despise the religion as now set forth. (Chartham X. 1. 4. 20v).

254 The wife of William Bell left church at the singing of the psalms cursing and railing. She uses an unlawful book of prayers. (Holy Cross, Canterbury, X. 1. 3. 8v).

255 There was a cross borne at the burial of Mother Cosen from Mr. Brent's house, to which the cross was returned. (Willesborough, X. 1. 2. 57v). Referred to the Archbishop.

256 Thomas Brakingbury and five others, though warned to the contrary, rang the bells on All Saints' Day after Evening Prayer. (Wye, X. 1. 3. 107v, 108r). They are to declare their fault on the following Sunday. Brakingbury refused to confess and was ordered to appear before the Queen's Commissioners. He appeared and was ordered to make declaration with the others.

257 Thomas Smyth and Henry Lodge churchwardens are to certify the names of those who celebrated the feast of Corpus Christi. (Willesborough, Y. 2. 24. 85v, 89r, 91v). They said they were not able to certify.

258 Hugh Jones kept the Nativity of Our Lady and shut his shop windows (St. And Canterbury, X. 1. 3. 1r)

259 Richard Baylye and his son Robert are favourers of superstition. (Iwade, X. 1. 3. 143v, 144r). Robert denied. Purgation quarta manu.

260 Michael Smith and Robert Allyn are suspected of keeping certain monuments of idolatry. (Mersham, X. 1. 2. 1/52r)

261 Images were found under boards at St. Alphege Canterbury. (Y. 2. 24. 42r). Stace Colman had keys of North and West doors and was clerk and sexton. He agreed that images were found. He took them down. Purgation septima manu. The images were standing at the Queen's Visitation and were taken down since.

WITHOLDING CHURCH PROPERTY

There being no state payment to the poor, responsibility for them fell on the parish. The parishioners were, nominally at any rate, the same as the members of the church, since all were required to attend church. There were two sources for support of the poor, bequests of land, cattle, sheep, etc. or money, which had to be administered by the parish church authorities, or levies made by a general meeting of parishioners which could be enforced against any who would not pay. Such gifts and levies were also available for church repairs. These examples illustrate the variety of gifts and bequests and show action against those who witheld property or would not pay the assessment made on them.

It will be seen that there are claims of a number of gifts for lights, no doubt made in Queen Mary's time. They mostly appear in the first year or two of this period. There is a reference to the lights being now 'put down'.

Gifts for lights etc.

262 Roger Nower of Barham witholds from Wootton 8d a year given for finding a lamp (X. 1. 4. 53v, 54r) Marginal note: 'Ye Queen's title, solvit domine Regine'. Presentment repeated. (X. 1. 5. 122v)

LAYMEN AND THE CHURCH

263 William Hannynge received 6s 8d to find a taper, which at that time was called the singlemen's taper. (Horton, X. 1. 3. 82v)

264 Robert Whyte witholds lands in Chelchbourne field for maintenance of seven tapers. (Brook, X. 1. 2. 1/9r)

265 Nicholas Smythson has six ewes given for maintenance of the Paschal light, which he has held for fourteen years and keeps as his own. (Upper Hardres, X. 1. 2. 1/10r)

266 Joan Marshe widow of Kingston keeps a cow given for maintenance of Our Lady light. (Upper Hardres, X. 1. 2. 1/10v)

267 John Kete witholds 2s a year given for the finding of a lamp in the chancel levied out of a field of his. The writing is removed from the vestry by somebody unknown. (Benenden, X. 1. 2. 1/33v)

268 Joan wife of Robert Masters of Willesborough, while she was widow of John Lucas, gave 24s a year out of lands for keeping a light and as an obit for the poor. Her husband has got hold of the indenture from William Daye who was holding it for the parishioners. (Benenden, X. 1. 2. 1/33v) Did not appear, pronounced contumacious, etc.

269 Walter Robert witholds certain lands given for maintenance of a lamp to burn before the high altar, also lands for two torches to burn at mass every Sunday, which lands are in the hands of John (Cuden). (Goudhurst, X. 1. 2. 1/63r & v)

270 Thomas Lake of Bredgate (? = Bredgar) witholds 2s a year due to the church of Borden from his lands in Bredgar Street for maintenance of St. Nicholas light. This is behind since the lights were put down. (X. 1. 2. 151v, 152r). He denied and is to appear to answer the churchwardens.

271 Christopher Baker witholds 8 lb of wax due out of his lands and a barn of his each year and is 27 years behind. The sum agreed for arrears is not paid. (Tenterden, X. 1. 2. 1/35v)

Gifts for mass

272 John Pollard and William Pollard have a house and 20 acres of ground given for a 'yevell' and a mass and a dirge to be said for ever. (Womenswold, X. 1. 3. 99v)

273 Thomas Kyngsdowne witholds 6d a year given for finding a dirge. It has not been paid for two years. (Eastchurch, X. 1. 4. 128 Av, 129r) 'Concordia' (marked 'non est') Marginal note: to be cited.

Land etc.

274 Roger Peake of Sandwich witholds three rods of ground belonging to the church. (Sholden, X. 1. 2. 1/19r)

CHURCH LIFE IN KENT

275 Anthony Gurlynge witholds 2s a year also 5 acres of land given by the will of Roger Pawlen. (St. Lawrence, Thanet, X. 1. 4. 17v 18r). He agrees to pay the 2s but denies the rest. The Judge assigned to the churchwardens the duty of proceeding according to law*.

276 George Caldham, executor of Agnes Benshkyn, witholds bequest of a tenement and garden in Stour Street to be sold and the proceeds given to the poor of St. Mildred. (St. Mildred, Canterbury, X. 1. 5. 93v, 94r). He was directed to produce his account.

Repairs

277 John Mecott has 3 li given by Stephen Foule for repair of the way between church and street. (Ospringe, X. 1. 2. 1/45r)

278 The wife of Robert Balden, as widow and executrix of John Sweting, witholds 4 li he bequeathed for church repair and the poor. (Hartlip, X. 1. 3. 148v)

279 George Owen, late of Stodmarsh now of Wickhambreux, refused to pay his assessment for church repairs. (X. 1. 7. 94v, 95r, 110r) Churchwardens say he assessed himself at 10s. He denies this and says he will not pay. Adjourned for proof. 8 February; both sides produce three witnesses. 8 March: Costs agreed at 3 li 7s 7d.

280 Thomas Wood of All Saints Canterbury witholds the assessment made for him for repair of St. Peter's Church when he lived in the parish. (X. 1. 5. 87v, 88r). He appeared and paid the churchwardens in Court 12d. Dismissed. Marginal note: '8d' (?a fee)

Poor relief

281 William Streter has not paid 6s 8d given by the will of Mrs. Rand for the poor box. (St. George, Canterbury, X. 1. 5. 96v, 97r). He did not appear. Excommunicated. 12 July 1564. Appeared and absolved. He said Mrs. Rand died intestate and had made a deed of gift to him of all her lands. About 3 or 4 hours before her death he in the presence of the parson and Robert Shawe took out of his own purse 6s 8d and gave it to Mrs Rand asking her to deliver it to the poverty with her own hands. It was very early in the morning and no poverty could be there, so he took the noble back and after she was dead distributed it to the poor.

282 Alexander Harrison witholds 20s a year given by the will of William Gilbert for the poor of Lyminge. (Ashford, X. 8. 2. 64v, 65r). The will is disputed by Alexander Blechinden, so adjournment to 15 December was asked for and granted.

283 Thomas Mylls and Martyn Mylls withold a gelding given to the parish by Thomas Myles the elder. They are in strife about it and the poor may lose it. (Blean, X. 1. 3. 6v, 7r). They agree the legacy. To be certified before the Feast of the Annunciation.

*Presumably as an 'instance cause'.

LAYMEN AND THE CHURCH

284 Richard Taylor and John Grenested have not paid their duty towards relief of the poor. (Cranbrook, X. 1. 5. 168v, 170r). Taylor did not appear. Excommunicated.

285 Robert Carpenter & others will not pay towards the poor. (Bethersden, X. 1. 7. 19v, 20r). Tylly (the apparitor) certified that the matter had been settled by John Tufton, Justice of the Peace, and the parties have agreed to pay.

286 Roger Pett has not given to the poor for a whole year. (Ivychurch, X. 8. 2. 78v). He said that churchwardens agreed to discharge of this for his writing and keeping the church book etc. and to give him 12d. Judge directs this to be certified.

287 Simon Gilbert has not given to the poor for a whole year. (Ivychurch, X. 8. 2. 78v, 79r). Did not appear. Excommunicated.

288 John Danyell refuses to pay his assessment for the poor, only $\frac{1}{2}$d a week. He has held it for over three months. (Doddington, X. 1. 4. 118v, 119r). He admitted and was monished to pay and have this certified by the next (sitting) 5 May: Certified.

289 Richard Cole and others refuse to pay their accustomed relief for the poor. (Littlebourne, X. 1. 5. 98v, 99r). Churchwardens appeared and certified that they had received 10d.

290 John Rolf refuses to pay 6d a quarter for the poor. He occupies 80 acres. (Stelling, X. 1. 5. 99v, 100r). Monished to pay 2s a year at 6d a quarter.

291 Robert Spracklinge of St. Lawrence Thanet witholds legacies for the poor under the will of widow Cockling. (St. Peter Thanet, X. 1. 5. 115. 116r). He said he paid 6s 6d a year to the poor according to the will and for the last year has paid it to the churchwardens.

292 Joan widow of Robert Stoddard occupies two acres and should give bread to the poor but refuses. (Shepherdswell, X. 1. 5. 110v, 111r). She admitted that her husband had bought the two acres. Churchardens appeared and said that Robert Curle who owned the land 36 years ago gave a cake of wassall bread yearly. Judge monished Joan to prove the end of the custom.

Cows and sheep

293 Edward Merywether of Shepherdswell detains three milch cows, witholding them from the poor of Eythorne. (X. 1. 2. 1/17v, X. 8. 5. 60v, X. 1. 4. 40v, 41r). He heard said and believes there were three cows in his father's hands for relief of the poor. His confession is accepted and he is to give to the poor in accordance with his father's will and the Queen's Injunctions.

294 Edmond Nott has two cows and Richard Fowrde one. They failed to return these and offer 10s per cow, though delivery or 10s was at the choice of the church. Mr. Harpesfelde, late archdeacon, 'willed them' to pay 10s, but this was not a judgment in Court. (Stowting, X. 1. 2. 1/24r) Marginal note: In Archbishop's Visitation.

295 Nicholas Smytheson witholds a sheep belonging to the church and does not pay for it. (Upper Hardres, X. 1. 4. 23v, 24r). The churchwardens are to certify that they have come to terms.

296 Thomas Harnet of Kettenton in Nonington witholds a cow of Eythorne given to set up five prickets every Sunday before the Sacrament. (X. 1. 4. 40v, 41r). He appeared and gave an answer in writing.

297 John Bayley of Ewell witholds six ewes of Shepherdswell. The rent of 2s a year is sixteen years behind. (X. 1. 4. 42v, 43r)

298 Agnes wife of Ralph Wulgate and daughter of Richard Geffrey has 50s belonging to the church, viz 40s for three cows and 10s for 5 ewes. (Stalisfield, X. 1. 4. 116v, 117r). She did not appear. Excommunicated. 24 May 1563: She appeared, was absolved and ordered to appear at the next General Chapter at Faversham.

299 John Wood of Chislet witholds a cow belonging to Alkham (X. 1. 5. 116v, 117r). He admits he has a cow given for the lamp light of Alkham. Monished to hand over a milch cow to the churchwardens before the end of this month of May.

300 William Harpe of Bethersden witholds a cow from Lenham (X. 1. 7. 33v, 34r). Did not appear. Excommunicated. 7 February. Tylly (apparitor) certified that Harper had satisfied the churchwardens of Bethersden with a cow of his own.

301 John Perry is to account for certain ewes belonging to the church (Bekesbourne, X. 1. 5. 98v, 99r). He said he had received 2s 6d each for 7 ewes. Adjourned.

Grain

302 Thomas Gannte of Ringwould has witheld for three years half a seam of barley given for repair of the church of Ripple. (X. 1. 4. 44v, 45r). Did not appear. Contumacious, penalty reserved.

303 Gilbert Fremlyn and John Blande withold a bushel of wheat given for maintenance of the holy loaf. (Hartlip, X. 1. 4. 126v, 127r). Churchwardens appeared and asked for adjournment to the General Chapter.

304 John Whitfeld witholds a seam of barley. (Tilmanstone, X. 1. 5. 108v). He undertook to deliver before All Saints Day.

LAYMEN AND THE CHURCH

305 Andrew Harpesfeld of Barham witholds half a seam of barley from Wootton. (X. 1. 5. 121v)

Clerk's wages

306 John Clarke will not contribute to the poor box, repairs or clerk's wages (2d a quarter), having land of 52s a year. (Minster Sheppey, X. 1. 7. 142v, 143r). He said he had offered 1d a quarter according to the custom of the house. He is to appear at the next General Chapter.

307 Davy Gibbes will not pay the clerk's wages as he did in the past (Holy Cross Canterbury, X. 1. 5. 87v, 88r). He appeared and agreed he was accustomed to pay 16d a year and of his own will made it 2s 7d a year. He understands now that his yard and close are outside the parish of Holy Cross. Judge ordered that two parishioners were to view the premises to see which part is most worth and he is to pay accordingly.

308 John Owen will not pay the clerk's wages, also annoys by keeping swine in the churchyard. (St. Mary Bredin, Canterbury, X. 1. 5. 88v, 89r). Appeared and was monished to pay 'drag' to the clerk.

Tithes*

309 Richard Borowe of Holy Cross Canterbury witholds tithe of a certain orchard for which he has hitherto paid. (St. Peter Canterbury, X. 1. 5. 87v, 88r). He says he paid 22d tithe for it to Margaret Ovingdon last Easter. She and the parson are interpleading for it at present. Dismissed.

310 Mrs. Hinxhill witholds tithe for a garden at the rate of 10d of the noble which she paid before and now will pay only 8d. (St. Peter Canterbury, X. 1. 5. 87v, 88r). She appeared and agreed to pay.

Miscellaneous

311 Richard Pantry, churchwarden last year, witholds certain goods. (Walmer, X. 1. 5. 112v, 113r). He produced a bill which the Judge taxed at 4s 4d and monished him to deliver the paten of the chalice and take 4s 4d from them.

312 William Rygden of Elham, Vincent Nethersole of Kingston and Robert Sloden of Lyminge withold certain duties belonging to the church of Elham. (X. 1. 5. 121v, 122r) Rygden and Sloden agree to pay (no entry against Nethersole).

313 John Chapman, executor of Robert Spechele, executor of his father Thomas, witholds 40s bequeathed by Thomas Spechele, half for sawing timber and half for setting up the church. He also bequeathed a cloth for the Communion table. (Wingham, X. 8. 2. 50v, 51r) Adjourned.

---

*Disputes on tithes would normally be instance causes at the suit of the person claiming the tithes.

314 Thomas Bull and John Shipton have not fulfilled the will of Bartholomew Peter who bequeathed 20 li to poor maidens married in the parish. (St. George, Canterbury, X. 1. 4. 1r). They are to account for the good of both man and woman.

315 Alex Mynge of Dover keeps away the churchyard of Charlton and makes pasture of it. (X. 1. 4. 49v, 50r). Contumacious. Penalty reserved.

316 We have only received the relief from the parsonage (20s a year) once in seven years. The fault is in the Chapter House of Canterbury. (Stone-in-Oxney, X. 1. 4. 63v, 64r). Marginal note: impropriated.

317 Lawrence Baker witholds 26s 8d given by the will of John Drey. (Bapchild. X. 1. 4. 124v, 125r). He lives in another diocese.

WITCHCRAFT

Following a papal bull in 1484 there was much persecution of witches on the Continent, particularly by the Inquisition. However, in this country witchcraft was regarded more as a statutory offence*, a felony punishable by death, than an ecclesiastical offence of heresy. The church courts did take notice of it with a view to excommunicating the offender.

The term witchcraft is used here to cover a number of different Latin terms applied to kindred offences (the 'crimen' being entered in Latin) maleficium, veneficium (implying originally the use of poison or potions), incantaciones, necromancia, ars magica.

It will be noted that these cases are nearly all entered in the act books (X. 8. 5. and Y. 2. 24) rather than in Visitation detecta records.

There are quite a number of cases, under these headings which give no detailed information of the nature of the witchcraft, though they may say something of the sentence.

318 Katherine Dalham wife of John D of Charing for incantations etc. (Y. 2. 24. 33v, 37r)

319 Elizabeth Webbe of Gt. Chart for incantations. (Y. 2. 24. 36v)

320 Joan Martyn of Waltham for incantations. (Y.2. 24. 41r) Purgation decima manu. Did not appear. Excommunicated.

321 Elizabeth Wynter of Teynham. (Y. 2. 24. 75r, 88v) for incantation. Purgation septima manu.

322 Robert Fisher of Ruckinge and wife for ars magica and incantations. (X. 8. 5. 23v, Y. 2. 24. 26r). Purgation septima manu for both. He failed and was excommunicated. She was referred to Consistory Court and purgation was ordered undecima manu.

---

*33 Hy VIII, c.8, repealed by 1 Edw VI, c.12, section 3, which repealed all felonies from 1 Hy VIII. Reenacted by 5 Eliz, c.16.

LAYMEN AND THE CHURCH

323 Joan Harper of Ashe for ars magica. (Y. 2. 24. 29r, 74v) Purgation septima manu. She failed in purgation and was ordered to do open penance in the market place of Canterbury and in the church of Sandwich and to make a declaration in the following form:

"I, Joan Harper, late of the parish of Ashe, detected before mine Ordinary for divers and sundry witchcrafts, sorceries and enchantments and thereof by law convicted, both by failing in my purgation and also by deposition of sundry witnesses. And now, willing to come to the unity of the church, here openly I do abjure, detest and abhor all witchcrafts, sorceries, and enchantments and generally arts magical and ungrammatical practices devised by the devil contrary to God's holy will. And I do promise hereafter never to use, practice or have in estimation any of the said unlawful arts or devilish practices. And further to manifest and disclose or detect from time to time during my life, as well myself and all such other that I shall know or understand to be practisers or offenders by any means in the same. So God me help and the holy Evangelists".

324 William Toppinden of Kenardington consented to the conveyance of Fisher's wife, a witch. (Y. 2. 24. 30v). Purgation quinta manu. Failed in purgation and excommunicated. Later submitted and absolved.

325 Alice Potten of Headcorn. (X. 8. 5. 72v, 92v) Purgation quinta manu. Failed in purgation and did not appear further. Excommunicated.

326 Alice Boreman of Wye (X. 8. 5. 70v, 72r) Purgation septima manu. Could not attend through illness. Commission issued to Mr. Pott to take the purgation.

327 Margaret Wells of Mersham (X. 8. 5. 66v). Purgation quinta manu. Did not appear. Excommunicated. Later absolved and produced compurgators.

328 Henry Pantry of Lyminge for incantations and necromancy (X. 1. 6. 76r, Z. 3. 8. 155v, 156r) Purgation sexta manu accepted.

329 Alice Busshe of St. Lawrence, late of St. John's Thanet suspected as a witch (X. 1. 2. 1/8r, X. 8. 5. 56r, 58v). Purgation quinta manu. 19 June 1561. Penance ordered at Christ Church, Canterbury and in the public market place there. (70r) 3 July. Did not appear. 17 July Excommunicated. Failed in purgation. (76r) 30 July Penance reordered. 2 October. Did not appear. Excommunicated.

330 Ellys wife of William Peerne is a common 'purcyfannte' to go to witches for them that are sick. She took a child's water to Mother Robertes and answered that God had laid his hand upon the child so it could not escape. The child was dead before she returned. (Headcorn, X. 1. 3. 72v, 73r)

331 Nicholas Hardwyn prayed that one Seks of Lynsted should not live till Saturday night. A woman taught him the prayer. His wife objected to the house being searched by William Amys, who then had a cow grinding her teeth and foaming at the mouth. (Kingsdown, X. 1. 2. 1/50r)

332 Agnes Frencham widow and Joan Gore of Sutton Valence 'who have used the seve and the sheres'. (X. 8. 5. 94v)

333 Robert Brayne's wife came to Richard Vynall's house for herbs. When he refused, she went away angry and said he would repent it. Then he lost 8 hogs. She said she had plagued him for his offence. (Biddenden, X. 1. 3. 157v)

334 Robert Sherman als Page said he sold Robert Brayne's wife a bushel of grain and, bacause she did not have help quickly to put it on her back, the drink made from his grain began to seethe and in a little while a man might have drawn it to the top of the house at his finger's end. Symon Mason said Robert Brayne's wife came to his house to borrow a horse to go to a wedding. As he denied her, he lost two bullocks next night. (Biddenden, X. 1. 3. 157Av, 158r). Her neighbours had lost cattle (X. 1. 3. 156v). She is to show cause why she should not be excommunicated.

335 The wife of Henry Aldrett put confidence in (blank) Kytherell, a sinister physician, and received sorcery at the time of her travail in childbirth. (Headcorn, X. 1. 4. 91v)

336 Alice Haffenden als Moss is a user of charms 'in measuring fealing of sycke persons' and in telling how things lost should be found. (Cranbrook, X. 1. 4. 94v)

337 Alice wife of George Bowman of Newenden came to the house of Richard Kensham for furze and, because his wife had none, she departed angrily. Within two days a calf of his bleated and leapt unlike any calf and, after pining for two days, it died. The parents of a child she had at nurse took away the child and, as she had said, it died. (X. 1. 5. 162v, 163r)

338 Henry Cleygate of Headcorn, being asked if he could help anything by witchcraft, confessed that, praying by the help of a god, he could. He learnt it of his mother about sixteen years ago, also of Sir Thomas Saunders, priest of Sutton, ten or eleven years ago. (X. 8. 5. 72r). He was declared convicted. Did not appear. Excommunicated.

VI
DISCIPLINING OF PRIVATE LIVES

The Church seems to have acted as keeper of the peace, at any rate in the country parishes. Any form of disturbance from being 'unquiet' or telling tales to violent swearing or abuse could be the subject of presentment by the churchwardens to the Archdeacon's Court. Slander would normally be a personal action an 'instance' cause, but evidently, especially when combined with violence, it was treated as a sin. It must not, therefore, be thought that, because there are a few cases of slander mentioned here, it was not prevalent. One of the difficulties in making a selection of the depositions in instance causes at Winchester* was that such a large proportion were almost a standardised form of slander. It only needed one person to refer to another as a whore, bastard, cuckold etc. for an action to be brought in the Court.

Testamentary causes would normally be 'instance' causes. However, particularly with bequests for the poor or where the executor had not adhered to the undertaking in his oath, the subject could be raised by presentment of the churchwardens, in the former case responsible through the overseers for maintenance of the poor and in the latter as watchdogs over the honesty of the parishioners.

The main and marginal headings to the items following will give a general classification, but two or more of such classifications are often combined in the same entry. Moreover, the border line between several of them is not easy to define.

This section divides itself into two parts, the first part consists of items of general disturbance and the second of sexual offences from irregular marriages and suspicious living to incest and bigamy. Between the two have been sandwiched neglect of duty by executors.

GENERAL MISBEHAVIOUR

Teller of tales

339 Margaret wife of Thomas Lane is an eavesdropper and bearer of tales. (St. Mary Northgate, Canterbury, X. 1. 2. 1/2v). Purgation tertia manu. She is a common slanderer and railer on the churchwardens and sidemen, saying that they are procured knaves. (X. 1. 3. 5v, 6r). Purgation quarta manu. Compurgators produced in both cases.

---

*Winchester Consistory Court Depositions 1561-1602, by Arthur J. Willis (1960).

340 The wife of James Apprice is a sower of discord and a tale bearer. (St. Margaret Canterbury, X. 1. 3. '20v, 21r). Did not appear. Contumacious. Adjourned.

Unquiet woman

341 The wife of (blank) Wyncke is an unquiet woman. (Holy Cross, Canterbury, X. 1. 3. 8v, 9r). Purgation quarta manu and a monition to behave herself decently.

342 John Bachler's wife is an unquiet woman with her neighbours. (Lenham, X. 1. 2. 1/59v, X. 8. 5. 69v). Did not appear. To be cited viis et modis.

Railing

343 Margaret Revell is a foul railing woman and unquiet. (Harbledown, X. 1. 2. 1/4v). Purgation quarta manu. Compurgators produced.

344 The widow of William Wells railed on the Ordinary, saying that when they stood two or three in white sheets at Christ Church door 'he ys well, but I think the devil is in him who will tear his bones' (St. Mary Northgate Canterbury, X. 1. 3. 5v, 6r). Purgation quinta manu.

345 The wife of Alexander Dence is a contemner of priests and ministers. She railed on a preacher, Mr. Tompson, and called him a knave. (Cranbrook, X. 1. 3. 74v, 75r & v). Purgation quinta manu in the person of her husband. Commission to Mr. Fletcher to receive compurgators.

Ill rule

346 Richard Toppinden and wife keep ill rule in their house. (Headcorn, X. 1. 4. 90v, 91r). Did not appear.

Scolds

347 Agnes Wotton is a great scolder and swearer. (St. Dunstan Canterbury, X. 1. 2. 1/4r). Did not appear. Excommunicated. (X. 8. 5. 77r). Produced compurgators quinta manu.

348 Ann wife of Henry Paine and Elizabeth Druett are common scolds. (St. John Thanet, X. 1. 3. 17v, 18r). Ann was monished to behave in future. The curate informed of their reconciliation.

349 Mrs. Bartlet and Joan Harryson chide and scold in Service time. (St. Mary Northgate Canterbury, X. 1. 4. 7v, 8r) Adjourned.

Swearing

350 John Hethe and John Saare have boys who are shameful swearers and cursers. Though of lawful age they cannot say their Creed. (Newnham, X. 1. 2. 1/48v). Monished to behave and to contribute 10d to the poor box.

DISCIPLINING OF PRIVATE LIVES

351 John Nicholas of Orlestone is a common swearer and sower of discord. (Warehorne, X. 1. 3. 27v, 28r). He lay in wait to lay violent hands on the parson. (28v, 29r). He said he offered to fight but did not. Adjourned.

Abuse

352 John Deacon is an evil man and behaves unseemly towards the priest, telling him that he lied openly in the pulpit before all the people. (Shepherdswell, X. 1. 2. 1/18v).

353 Edward Carpenter, alderman, challenged the churchwardens that they were not bound by their oaths, being sworn at a disturbance ('inquiet') in the Town Hall. He called churchwarden Hopper a knave for demanding 6s 8d for the burial of his wife in the church. (St. Peter Canterbury, X. 1. 3. 3v)

354 William Blake after Evening Prayer fell out with the parson for speaking against great ruffs and breeches. He said the parson ought to speak only of parish matters and not of the Jews or the Pope. Though advised to revoke his words he refused to do so. He called the parson knave for declaring the Scriptures. (Warehorne, X. 1. 3. 27v, 28r) Purgation quarta manu. (29v, 30r). He told the parson that he said more in the pulpit than any honest man would say. Marginal note in both cases: he is dead.

355 Emery Wutton said that those who presented him were knaves and villains. (St. Dunstan Canterbury, X. 1. 3. 2v)

Slander

356 John Browne for slander of the wife of John Smyth, being an honest woman. (Dymchurch, X. 1. 5. 50v, 51r). The parties are reconciled. Dismissed.

357 John Fletcher and Margery his wife are slanderers of their neighbours and disquiet persons. She is a scold. (Boxley, X. 1. 3. 51v, 52r). Did not appear. Excommunicated. They appeared and were absolved. Purgation quarta manu for both. Compurgators produced (four for each).

358 Edward Holt is slanderous against proceedings of the Queen and a sower of contention between neighbours with great threatenings. (Ewell, X. 1. 3. 80v)

359 George Overy asked George Wood's boy where the knave his father and the whore his mother were.(Throwley, X. 1. 3. 136v, 137r). The vicar certified that peace was restored.

360 John Amounte slandered Richard Ford churchwarden (of Stowting) for saying he should have presented him (Amount) in Queen Mary's time. He accused Ford of treason. (Horton, X. 1. 5. 123v, 124r). He admitted it all. Paid 12d '....omnibus'

CHURCH LIFE IN KENT

361 Pyne's wife slandered Thomas Standen, saying that he had received certain lands contrary to the Queen's laws. (Hawkhurst, X. 1. 5. 164v). The Judge commissioned the curate to reform Pyne's wife.

362 Margaret Duston of St. Paul Canterbury for slandering priests. (X. 8. 5. 38r). She denied. Purgation sexta manu failed. Adjourned.

Blasphemy

363 Agnes wife of John Hake and the wife of Richard Starky are common scolds and blasphemers. (St. Mary Northgate Canterbury, X. 1. 2. 1/2r). Purgation tertia manu. Compurgators produced.

364 Peter Geffrye and Thomas Geffrye are common swearers and blasphemers. (Stalisfield, X. 1. 3. 128v, 129r). Thomas acknoledged the fault. He is to declare this before the parishioners and give 12d for the poor. Penance certified.

365 John Longeley butcher is a blasphemer of God and slanderer of his neighbours. (Faversham, X. 1. 2. 1/44r)

Drunkenness

366 Christopher Singleton is a drunkard. (St. Margaret Canterbury, X. 1. 3. 19v, 20r). He promised to reform. Monished to desist and pay 12d to the poor box.

367 Roger Fynch is a drunkard, but on admonition he does somewhat withdraw himself from that vice. (Tenterden, X. 1. 5. 154v, 155r).

368 William Clarke keeps ill rule in time of Service and drunkards in his house. (St. George Canterbury, X. 1. 5. 96v, 97r). He confessed that one Henry Fuller came to his house drunk on a Sunday in time of Service, but he would not go when required to. The churchwardens appeared and said he had drunkards several times in the house. Purgation quinta manu. (134r) Compurgators produced and satisfied.

369 Thomas Wood is a drunkard and works on the Sabbath. (St. Mary Northgate Canterbury, X. 1. 4. 7v, 8r). He has gone away.

370 John Clarke glover is a drunkard and seldom comes to church. (St. Mary Northgate, Canterbury, X. 1. 4. 7v, 8r). He is to acknowledge his fault.

371 Lynne Tayloure and Robert Blackbourne are common ale hunters in time of Service. (Chislet, X. 1. 2. 1/8v, X. 8. 5. 61v). Before the Archbishop.

372 Thomas Atkynson is a drunkard (St. George Canterbury, X. 1. 5. 96v, 97r). He denied. Purgation quinta manu. Failed in purgation.

DISCIPLINING OF PRIVATE LIVES

DUTY OF EXECUTORS

373 Joan Harnet, widow and executrix of her husband James, has not paid bequests to a poor maid's marriage and others, persuaded by Thomas Astone. (St. Lawrence Thanet X. 1. 2. 1/8r, X. 8. 5. 59r). Certified they are paid.

374 Thomas Bull and John Shipton have not fulfilled the will of Bartholomew Peter, who bequeathed 20 li to poor maidens married in the parish. (St. George Canterbury, X. 1. 4. 1r). Bull appeared and was instructed to prepare an account. Shipton did not appear. Adjourned.

375 Agnes Balden (now wife of John Sweting) as executrix of Robert Balden her husband witholds legacies of 2 li to the church and 2 li to the poor of Hartlip. (Harrietsham, X. 1. 5. 78v). Balden to be summoned, also John Sweting now living at East Sutton. (X. 1. 6. 49v). Alice (sic) did not appear. Excommunicated. (64v) She appeared and said that last Tuesday she paid 40s for the poor and 40s for repairs according to the will of her husband late of Rainham. She was absolved and is to pay 5 marks to the church of Rainham. (72v) John Sweting appeared. He is to prove payment of the 5 marks.

376 Dr. Bonner, late Bishop of London, as executor of Mr. Myllinge late parson of Chartham, holds his bequest of 10 li for mending highways. (Chartham, X. 1. 2. 1/11r).

377 Richard Cowper has not fulfilled the will of John Liverocke to lay certain loads of stone on the highways. (Ashford, X. 1. 2. 1/30v) To be done by St. John Baptist Day next.

378 Henry Horslye of Harbledown and Vincent Hall of Hackington, executors of John Androw, withold certain goods he gave for repair of highways. (Hackington, X. 1. 3. 21v, 22r). They are to render account at the next sitting after Easter.

379 Francis Wylford gentleman witholds money bequeathed for mending the highway between Northiam (Sussex) church and Gollett's Cross in Sandhurst (Sandhurst, X. 1. 3. 58v).

380 William Toppinden, of Benchechilde and now of New Romney, witholds without legal authority certain goods of his brother who died at Kenardington. (Kenardington, X. 1. 2 1/53v, X. 8. 5. 68r) Adjourned. (72v, 73r) 2 July 1561. He said he had not yet administered. He is to appear and show cause why he should not be punished. 31 July. Did not appear. Excommunicated. 16 October. He appeared and said he had had all his brother John's goods delivered to him before John's death. He was monished to give proof. 13 November. Distribution was certified. Dismissed, unless the relict wished to prosecute the matter.

CHURCH LIFE IN KENT

381 William Whetland and Joan Longe alias Whetland his wife
for accounts as administrators of the estate of John Staple junior.
(X. 1. 5. 133r). Deposition of John Block of Lynsted who said
that one Gyles Staple came to him and said he was John Staple
senior's brother. (135r) Account produced.

382 John Block for accounts as administrator of the estate of John
Staple senior of Lynsted. (X. 1. 5. 135r, 178v). To prove payment of 30 li exhibition of John Staple junior, son of John Staple
senior, at the City of London Grammar School. (X. 1. 6. 54v,
55r). Remitted from Prerogative Court of Canterbury to show
cause why he should not be charged with 30 li. (58r & v) Proctor
for Henry and Richard Staple as administrators. (75r) Witnesses
for Henry and Richard Staple. (87r, 89v, 96r & v) Administration granted to Giles Staple, John Norden and John Butler. John
Block and his proctor declared contumacious. (96v, 97r & v,
98r & v, 99r) Will of John Staple senior and grant to Henry and
Richard Staple (full texts). (99r & v) Conveyance of goods and
chattels of John Staple senior by Henry and Richard Staple to
John Block.

383 Thomas Pattinden has a legacy given to the highways by William
Peers and has married his widow. (Goudhurst, X. 1. 3. 46v,
47r). He did not appear and was declared contumacious.

IRREGULARITY IN MARRIAGE

Without banns

384 John Dixon and Agnes Frost widow were married in London without
banns. (Faversham, X. 1. 2. 1/44r)

385 William Becher and Elizabeth Ellett were married without banns.
(Boughton Monchelsea, X. 1. 2. 1/60v)

386 Thomas Man said openly that he was married without banns in our
parish.(Cheriton, X. 1. 3. 78v)

Banns called, but no marriage

387 John Pottyn and Agnes Collens. Banns were called three times but
John refuses marriage. (Rolvenden, X. 1. 4. 82v, 83r). Certified that they are married.

388 George Lynleye widower and Denys Knowles spinster. Banns were
called three times but not married. (Rolvenden, X. 1. 4. 82v,
83r). Certified by curate and parishioners that they are married.

Marriage out of own parish

389 Frances Cortys and William Chalborne were married out of the
parish. (Faversham X. 1. 3. 132v, 133r). Cortys referred to
Consistory Court. Chalbourne 'non est talis' (? there is not such
a man)

DISCIPLINING OF PRIVATE LIVES

390   John Amonte (Mownte) curate of Horton was married out of the parish without banns or licence. (X. 1. 5. 123v, 124r). He said he had answered for the offence at the Archbishop's Visitation. Monished to produce the judicial act.

391   John Nethersole was married out of the parish and out of time, banns not being asked. (Tenterden, X. 1. 2. 1/36r)

Taking Communion on marriage

392   William Ashday and his wife Agnes did not receive Communion on the day of their marriage. (X. 8. 5. 24v) He said it was only the fault and negligence of the curate. Adjourned.

393   Thomasine Barnard and John Welby of Harrietsham refused Communion on marriage. (X. 8. 5. 24v) He admitted it and said they did not because the curate had already celebrated mass. Monished to conform better to the unity of the church.

Place of marriage unknown

394   Elizabeth Crayford is with child by Andrew Crayford whom she has married. (Cranbrook, X. 1. 5. 169v) She is to produce evidence of where she was married and to whom (? to be purified) and to show this to the vicar of Cranbrook.

HUSBAND AND WIFE LIVING APART

395   Katherine wife of Anthony Moswell for not keeping company with her husband. (St. Andrew Canterbury, X. 1. 2. 1/5v) Certified they are reconciled. (Newington by Sittingbourne, Y. 2. 24. 36r) 11 November 1560. She did not appear for purgation. Excommunicated.

396   Jude Herne lives away from his wife and is strongly suspected of being with another woman. (Bearsted, X. 1. 2. 65v)

397   James Godding lives apart from his wife, it is not known whose fault. (Halstow, X. 1. 2. 1/43v). He is dead.

398   The wife of John Tanner has been apart from her husband for a long time. (Brenzett, X. 1. 3. 33v, 34r). She said her husband left her without her consent.

399   James Awsten lives apart from his wife. (Boughton Aluph, X. 1. 3. 104v, 105r). He said they had separated by consent, only owing to poverty.

400   Thomas Tolherste and his wife for living apart and dividing their goods by indenture. (Headcorn, X. 1. 4. 90v, 91r). He appeared and confirmed that they were together and live honestly.

401   Joan Smeth lives apart from her husband, (Appledore, X. 1. 3. 30Av, 31r). The curate certified he had denounced her according to the mandate. He was commissioned to absolve her as she is detained by illness.

402 Roger Hewet put away his wife without a cause. (Headcorn, X. 1. 4. 90v, 91r). He was ordered to take his wife again and then to appear again. A further charge of carnal knowledge of Elizabeth Toppinden in the house of Alexander Fishcocks. He is to submit to be examined. (X. 1. 5. 175v, 176r) His wife will not keep company with him, alleging that she loves Robert Humfry better. They were monished to live together and be reconciled.

LIVING SUSPICIOUSLY

403 Bartholomew Sandy keeps a wench and goes about the country with her. (St. Dunstan Canterbury, X. 1. 2. 1/3r). Did not appear. Excommunicated. Absolved. Purgation quinta manu. Compurgators produced.

404 Richard Norberye ran away with another man's wife. (Seasalter, X. 1. 2. 1/7v). Marginal note:* Excommunicated. (X. 8. 5. 58r) He was with Beatrice Stanford of Seasalter. Did not appear. Excommunicated.

405 Leonard Spracklynge lives suspiciously with Julyan Saunder widow. (St. Lawrence Thanet, X. 1. 2. 1/7v, X. 8. 5. 58v). 1561 Certified that banns were published and that they would be married (Y. 2. 24. 73v, 98r) May - September 1562. Adjourned. (X. 1. 7. 114v, 115r). He admits banns were called three times, but said this presentment was not due to real suspicion but was made offensively and he intends to prove this. Adjourned for the proof.

406 Richard Miller is suspected with the wife of Richard Apthomas (Kenardington, X. 1. 3. 26v, 27r). Purgation septima manu. Failed in purgation. Excommunicated. Submitted and absolved 'ad cantelam'. Purgation repeated. Produced six but two refused. Penance ordered and he was not to hold converse with the woman.

407 Thomas Stonestreete senior and Margaret Trusnothe of Bethersden live suspiciously together, Margaret being his wife's sister. (Y. 2. 24. 112v). 5 November 1563. Evidence that Margaret entered his house suspiciously. Purgation for him sexta manu. She did not appear. Excommunicated. (116r, 120r) He was ill and his purgation deferred. She appeared petitioning absolution. Purgation sexta manu. (121r) Thomas still ill. Adjourned. (125r) Both failed to appear. Excommunicated. Commission to curate of Halden to receive penance and absolve him. (131r) 5 May 1564. His penance certified and he is dismissed. (This entry is scored through).

---

*Such a marginal note is probably made against the detecta entry from the later action recorded in the act book (X. 8. 5.), so that this does not mean that he was excommunicated twice.

DISCIPLINING OF PRIVATE LIVES

408 Thomas Mos and Dorothy Wilson. Their banns were called three times but they are not married. She is suspected of keeping ill rule with another. She confesses the priest had 4s for the Commissionary's fee for divorce* of the said parties. (Rainham, X. 1. 2. 1/46v)

409 Henry Lawe of Sittingbourne has taken away a maid from the parish who was servant to Thomas Nethersole. No banns or marriage. (Milton by Sittingbourne, X. 1. 2. 1/48r) Marginal note: They are married.

410 George Tofts and Katherine Moswell 'resorting together of crime and yvill rule keeping' (St. Andrew Canterbury, under Philip Lewes, X. 1. 3. 1v, X. 8. 5. 43r). On New Year's Day (1560/1 they came out of Scot's house suspiciously. Y. 2. 24 100r & v) 13 October 1562. Katherine of St. Peter Canterbury did not appear. Excommunicated. (Y. 2. 24 102r) Tofts produced his case in writing. Purgation septima manu. (Z. 3. 8. 84r) 15 October 1562. Katherine did not appear. Excommunicated. (Y. 2. 24. 104v) 24 November. Katherine appeared. Purgation septima manu. 8 December. She did not appear. Excommunicated. (Y. 2. 24. 105r) 10 December. She was absolved and produced compurgators. They refused, so she failed in purgation. Monished not to consort with Tofts except in church or public market place. If she should happen to be in a house where Tofts is, she must leave.

411 Widow Scudder (wife of Robert Sanders scored through) went away with George Bakester of Brookland and has now returned. (Brenzett, X. 1. 3. 33v, 34r). They confessed. He is to do penance on three Sundays in his own church and she in her own church any Sunday with bare feet until she is firm in her penitence.

412 Ann Grene a single wench abiding with our curate and great with child. (Biddenden, X. 1. 3. 64v, 65r). Did not appear. Excommunicated. Marginal note: At Flimwell (Sussex)

413 John Reignold of St. Mildred Canterbury for suspicious association with Agnes Wood. (X. 1. 6. 34r, 80r). Monished not to associate with her except in public places. (91r) For purgation quinta manu. Did not appear and declared convicted. (101r). They were monished not to live together. To do penance next Sunday in their parish church. (109v) They will do no penance as they are man and wife. Declared contumacious and excommunicated. (121r & v, 122r, 157r) Her husband Richard Powell died on 24 July last and is buried in the churchyard of St. Bride, London. Thomas Feen of St. Bride deposes. (X. 1. 7. 79v, 80r) Process is in the ex officio act book of 1565*.

---
*Divorce could only be from bed & board ('a mensa et thoro'), little more than a judicial separation. Full divorce ('a vinculo matrimonii') would only be obtainable for marriage within the prohibited degrees of affinity, which would be null and void ab initio.
**i.e. X. 1. 6, referred to above.

CHURCH LIFE IN KENT

HARBOURING THOSE UNDER SUSPICION

414 John Barnarde keeps a woman with child in his house, the father is unknown. (Seasalter, X. 1. 3. 13v, 14r) 27 February 1561/2. Did not appear. Excommunicated. 11 March. He appeared and said Ann, a tall woman, was brought to bed of a female child about Shrovetide and left him in Lent. Absolved.

415 Richard Harenden having Alice Wyggshill a midwife in his house. (X. 8. 5. 116r) He admitted it and was to do penance in his parish church. Penance was certified by the vicar of Marden.

416 Derick Cornelys, tailor, for keeping a suspected person. He has been monished to put her away and would not. (E Langdon, X. 1. 2. 1/19r, Y. 2. 24 38v). He and Alice Mathue appeared and promised they would be married. To be certified at the next sitting after the marriage.

417 Robert Fowle brought Jane Fawkner from beyond London, who was delivered of a child and kept in his house till after christening and churching and she is gone. (Benenden, X. 1. 2. 1/33r)

418 Andrew Gosfrithe of Boughton Aluph for having a woman with child in his service who has gone away. (X. 8. 5. 97v). Monished to produce her. Did not appear. Adjourned. Marginal note: (? he) is dying.

419 Thomas Overy as a woman Joan was brought to bed in his house with a female child, whose father she says is Henry Tirrey of Eastwell. (Molash, X. 1. 5. 101v, 102r). She is excommunicate. He appeared. (102v) (blank). Frenche of Eastwell is a maintainer of the said naughtiness.

420 William Skamberlane for harbouring fornicators and midwives. (X. 8. 5. 117r). He admitted it and was to do penance in his parish church. He did not appear. Excommunicated. He appeared, petitioned for absolution and was absolved. Marginal note: Paid 2s 4d. He was to do penance in the church of Marden according to a written confession handed to him. His tears were apparently accepted as his penance 'deinde dominus, ex gratia mera percipiens ex lacrimis eis (?eius) peniten (ciam), ...ab ulteriori etc.

INCONTINENCE

421 Margaret Greneway of St. Mary Bredin Canterbury for incontinence. (X. 8. 5. 2r). She denied. Purgation septima manu failed. To do penance next Sunday at the Cathedral. Did not appear. Excommunicated.

422 Thomas Barnet of St. Mary Bredin for incontinence with Margaret Greneway. (X. 8. 5. 2v). He agreed he had said that he had had carnal knowledge of her, but in fact he had not. Purgation septima manu. He did not appear so was declared convicted. Adjourned for him to hear sentence of excommunication.

DISCIPLINING OF PRIVATE LIVES

423   John Dave for incontinence with Bennet Grenfeld who died in child-bed and said he was the father. (Appledore, X. 1. 3. 30Av, 31r). He did not appear. Excommunicated.

424   Leonard Norgrave had a servant in his house that went away with child and has come back. (St. Andrew Canterbury, X. 1. 2. 1/5v) Incontinence with his servant. (St. Mary Bredman Canterbury, X. 8. 5. 86v). He undertook to marry her. (St. Mary Bredin Canterbury, Y. 2. 24. 73v). He had married her. Dismissed.

425   Nicholas Nycolson of Bilsington and Margaret wife of Thomas Smyth of Orlestone for incontinence. (Orlestone, X. 1. 3. 32v, 33r). For him purgation quinta manu and he was monished not to associate with her except in public places. He confessed he had been there twice since (?the presentment) and was monished to declare his fault before the parishioners. Thomas Smyth appeared and said he had been advised by parishioners to warn Nycolson but did not do so. He was monished to declare his fault before the parishioners. Margaret appeared. Purgation quinta manu.

426   John Pottet of Rolvenden for incontinence with his servant. (X. 8. 5. 48v). He confessed and is to do penance on the three following Sundays and in the public market place of Cranbrook. (93r). Excommunicated. (95r) Absolved and purgation ordered. Certified that he has left the diocese.

427   Thomas Butts of Rainham for incontinence with Alice Turner. (X. 8. 5. 13r). He said Alice was in his house as a servant for half a year. She came of her own will. Asked if she came for pay or for love, he said for love. There was no arrangement for wages. Chapman, the apparitor, deposed that there was 'fame'* in the parish of their incontinence. Purgation septima manu. He did not appear so failed in purgation. 26 April. He appeared and said that he and the said Isabel (sic) have contracted for marriage** and live as husband and wife. He was monished that marriage was to be solemnized and certified.

FORNICATION

428   Henry Judson for fornication with his maid Faith Hancocke. (Frittenden, X. 1. 3. 70v, 71r). He confessed and is to do three penances in public places in Cranbrook, Maidstone and Ashford and in his church next Sunday. Penance certified by the curate.

---

*A word that appears commonly at this time. No doubt it is based on the Latin 'fama' but has more than its original meaning of 'rumour', rather public opinion (mostly in a derogatory sense).

**For precontracts of marriage see 'Marriage Contracts or Espousals in the reign of Queen Elizabeth' by A. Percival Moore (Associated Architectural Societies' Reports and Papers, 1909, vol. xxx, part 1, p. 261.

429 George Brygs has got John Comes' widow with child in Sussex and she is kept there at his cost. His wife is at Bodiam. (Sandhurst, X. 1. 2. 1/29v, X. 1. 5. 163r). John (sic) Briggs and Comes' widow ran out of the parish leaving his wife behind and have now come back: he works at Newenden. Churchwardens of Newenden ordered to monish Briggs to appear.

430 John Ungley of Sandhurst had a child by Margaret Bearde of this parish. She is now dead, but he is unpunished. (Cranbrook, X. 1. 2. 1/32r).

431 Elizabeth Bargrave of Willesborough is with child at John Bent's. She was brought from Willesborough by Richard Thornton. (Bilsington, X. 1. 2. 1/52r, X. 8. 5. 67r, 92v). Thornton said she was with child by Robert Torfet of Chartham a servant of Robert Stede of Hinxhill. She did not appear. Excommunicated.

432 Elizabeth Senoke has had a child by one Cortope or by her brother's servant Thomas. (Goudhurst, X. 1. 3. 47v, 48r, X. 8. 5. 98v). She has left. Certificate of her confession produced. Cortope appeared for not producing the woman, declared contumacious and penalty deferred.

433 Alice Blake of Brookland for fornication with Robert Crewse. (X. 8. 5. 14v). To do penance next Sunday in the church of Brookland with an outer garment of linen and a white rod held in her hand during the time of Divine Service. He appeared and confessed to adultery with Alice and was ordered to do penance. (19r). His penance at Brookland certified. To do further penance at New Romney. Penance certified.

434 Dionisia Hugh and James Austen of Staplehurst for fornication. (X. 8. 5. 15r & v). She confessed she was with child by him. He appeared and denied and was ordered purgation septima manu. She was to attend the purgation. She confessed fornication with one Darknall of Frittenden by persuasion and order of Austen after she was with child by Austen. Austen appeared and confessed that Joan Batherst, a servant of his, was with child in his house ten years ago. He failed in purgation and was ordered penance in his parish church next Sunday and in the market place of Maidstone on the Thursday after Easter. A similar penance for her. He did not appear and was excommunicated. (19r). Her penance certified and she is to do further penance at Staplehurst. (39r). He produced compurgators and three women to whom she had confessed that the child was not Austen's. (79v) 1 October 1560. He was ordered penance, refused, was pronounced contumacious and excommunicated. Marginal note: Decreed that 'significavit' was to issue. (81r). Full text of certificate of Archbishop dated 28 October 1560 that he had been purged in the Archbishop's Visitation. (85r). Letter from Archbishop (full text in English) of 27 October 1561 including instruction to proceed according to law against James Austen to keep the child and relieve the parish of its charge.

DISCIPLINING OF PRIVATE LIVES

435 John Harenden for fornication with his servant Alice Wiggshill. (X. 8. 5. 115v). Did not appear. Excommunicated. Appeared and submitting was absolved. To do penance on the Feast of the Purification in the church of Frittenden and on the following Sunday in the church of Marden. He humbly petitioned for commutation as to the white garment. The Judge decreed that he should do his penance without the white garment, but should give for the poor in the presence of his neighbours 6s 8d on that day, 6s 8d on St. John Baptist Day and 6s 8d on Michaelmas Day. Further, he was to give to the poor box of Marden on that day 3s 4d and a further 3s 4d on St. John Baptist Day. And further, he was not to associate with the woman except in public places, e. g. church or the market place and he was to provide from his own funds for the maintenance of the child. 13 April 1564. He did not appear. Excommunicated.

WHOREDOM

436 John Coppin is a common whoremonger. He has one churched about three weeks ago and another brought to bed. (Minster Thanet, X. 1. 3. 22r, 23r). 27 February. Excommunicated. 28 March. Appeared and absolved. (X. 8. 5. 82r, 83r). He is to produce the woman. The woman is now in child bed. He said William his 'thressher' was the man and he undertook to prove it. He is to produce the other woman after she has given birth, under pain of excommunication.

437 Alys wife of Richard Rawkyns is suspected of whoredom and receives suspicious persons in her house, such as William Mylles of Cranbrook and Thomas Mylles of Newenden. (Cranbrook, X. 1. 4. 94v, 95r). Did not appear. Excommunicated. (X. 1. 5. 38v, 39r). She left the parish and has come back. She did not appear. Excommunicated.

438 John Strycklande and Margaret Mabye for whoredom. He confessed, saying he had another wife beyond London. (St. Mary Northgate, Canterbury, X. 1. 3. 6v, 7r). Purgation quinta manu for her. She failed and was declared convicted. He failed to appear, was declared contumacious. Penalty reserved.

439 William Mallom for whoredom with Lowe's wife. (Burmarsh, X. 1. 3. 30v, 30Ar). He has left the parish. She did not appear and was excommunicated.

440 Elizabeth Anthony for whoredom. (Upchurch, X. 1. 3. 146v, 147r). She did not appear and was excommunicated. Later she appeared and was ordered to reconcile herself publicly with the parishioners.

441 John Pottyte a married man for enticing Joan Iden, wife of William Iden, to whoredom. William found John in his bedchamber. (Rolvenden, X. 1. 2. 1/32v).

ADULTERY

442 Richard Mallynson of Holy Cross Canterbury had a wench with child. (St. Dunstan Canterbury, X. 1. 2. 1/3v). Adultery with Julian Mason of Faversham. (X. 8. 5. 86v). To do penance at Christ Church Canterbury on Christmas Day. (Y. 2. 24. 33r). She has fled.

443 Matthew Warden for adultery and fornication with the wife of Richard Frend of Holy Cross. (St. Peter Canterbury, X. 1. 2. 1/3r). Purgation sexta manu. (X. 8. 5. 86r). Appeared and adjourned. Did not appear further. Excommunicated.

444 William Tolherst of Hawkhurst had carnal knowledge of a married woman at Cranbrook. (X. 8. 5. 49r, 87r). He admitted it five years ago and was in prison for eleven weeks for it. She was the wife of a certain Chandler. He was to produce two others to prove he had not known her since and was absolved.
(X. 1. 4. 135v, 136r). Excommunicated on charges of adultery drunkenness and blasphemy.

445 Thomas Crafthorne, a married man, had a child in adultery with Marion Wood. He has fled to Warbleton, Sussex, as servant to Mr. Cheyney. (Rolvenden, X. 1. 2. 1/32v, X. 8. 5. 47v). She appeared and confessed. To do penance on three Sundays and in the market place of Cranbrook. He has left the parish. (93v). He is excommunicated. The woman has done penance.

446 Harry Olyver of Kingsnorth for adultery with widow Hale. (Halden, X. 1. 2. 1/37r). Marginal note: Excommunicated.*
(X. 8. 5. 66v). Purgation septima manu. Did not appear. Excommunicated. (93r). Petitioned for absolution. Absolved subject to purgation quinta manu.

447 William Newstrete and the wife of James Odyarne (Odyam) are suspected of adultery. (Ashford, X. 1. 3. 66v, 67r). February 1561/2. He denied. Purgation quinta manu. 13 April. He produced three compurgators. Monished not to associate with the woman and to acknowledge his fault according to a schedule (of penance). (X. 1. 4. 72v, 73r). Purgation accepted.
(X. 8. 5. 109r) December 1562. He denied. Purgation quinta manu. (110v). 11 February 1562/3. Compurgators produced and accepted.

448 Thomas Bonne (Bowne) having a wife got his servant with child five or six years ago 'the parish being much aggrieved by that heinous sin and that hitherto there hath not been known any punishment for the same to the quieting of the parish'. (Biddenden, X. 1. 5. 44v, 45r). He prayed for the benefit of the Queen's indulgence. Adjourned.

*See footnote on page 48

DISCIPLINING OF PRIVATE LIVES

449 Robert Dewar lives in adultery with Barbara Stire his harlot. (Ashford, X. 1. 2. 1/30r, X. 8. 5. 7r). Purgation septima manu failed. Did not appear. Excommunicated. (X. 8. 5. 11v, 12r). Evidence of Margaret and Robert Robinson. (63v). Absolved but monished to treat his wife matrimonially and not to associate with the woman. (Y. 2. 24. 4v). Living apart from his wife Mary (54v) Absolved.

450 Barbara Stere of Ashford widow for adultery with Robert Dewar. (X. 8. 5. 7v). Did not appear. Excommunicated. (47v). She appeared and confessed. To do penance on three Sundays and in the market place of Cranbrook. He has left the parish.

451 William Saunder for adultery with a woman kept in his house. (Harbledown, X. 1. 2. 1/4r, X. 8. 5. 77v). Penance ordered next Sunday in Christ Church and in the market place of Canterbury, on the following Sunday in the market place of Ashford and on the following Thursday in the market place of Maidstone. 2 October. Did not appear. Excommunicated. 16 November. Absolved on undertaking to do penance. (Y. 2. 24. 53r) May 1561. Appeared with Agnes Parrett and admitted being father of her child. He had promised her marriage but on condition, a year ago, that she produced a testimonial. As he was arrested he confessed that he would marry her, giving her a piece of gold and kissing her. (58r, 73r. 74r). Saunder of Blean appeared and admitted he had not married Agnes Barrett as ordered. Asked if he would produce her, he said no. Declared contumacious and excommunicated. Referred to Archbishop. He said many others had had to do with Agnes Barrett and was ordered to report their names. Vicar of Blean had denounced him last Sunday as excommunicated. (76v). They had contracted for marriage and he undertook that marriage would be solemnized in the face of the church. He was absolved.

452 Peter London for adultery with his servant Joan. (Patrixbourne, X. 1. 2. 1/12v, Y. 2. 24. 39r). To do penance on two following Sundays in the Cathedral. On his petition the Judge amended this to paying 6s 8d to the poor box next Sunday with a white wand in his hand declaring his guilt and 6s 8d to the poor box of Patrixbourne on the following Sunday in the same way.

453 Joan Neame of Woodnesborough for adultery with Robert Stile of Sandwich (X. 8. 5. 6v). She denied. Purgation (double) septima manu, six women from Woodnesborough and six from Sandwich. She produced twelve, all from Woodnesborough. Asked why there were none from Sandwich, she said she had asked none. Six from Sandwich were produced (?refused on oath), so purgation failed and she was convicted. To appear to show cause why she should not be excommunicated. (11r). Peter Lylly appointed proctor. (32v). Remitted from the Court of Arches. (33r). To appear to show cause why she shall not be excommunicated. Did not appear. Excommunicated.

454 John Ogar (Awgor) for adultery with Julian wife of Edward Baker. (Folkestone X. 1. 5. 117v, 118r, 128v). He did not appear. Ex-

communicated. She appeared and denied. Purgation quarta manu. Later, he appeared and denied and was pronounced contumacious. Curate of Folkestone to be written to that excommunication stands. Baker, husband of Julian, appeared with letters missive from the Mayor of Folkestone and others. Julian's purgation deferred.

455 Agnes Wytherden of Harbledown for adultery with George Nynne of Thanington. (X. 1. 6. 87v). Excommunication ordered. (84v). Nynne demanded articles in writing. The Judge refused to let him see them before examination. He went away, was declared contumacious and excommunicated. (88r) 31 October 1565. Sentence of excommunication (in full)* (X. 1. 7. 77v, 78r). Process is in the 1565 Act Book:** (92v). Purgation decima*** manu, six women of Harbledown and four from the house of the Brothers of Harbledown (101v, 102r). Compurgators produced, but only five would take the oath. Adjourned. (130v, 137r) To do penance next Sunday in the Chapter House at Canterbury 'loco conc(il)ionibus assignato tempore conc(il)ionis' (? = at a meeting of the General Chapter), wearing a white linen vestment and holding a white rod in her hand and then to appear again for an order for further penance. Appeal to the Court of Arches.

456 Humphrey Gaskoyn of All Saints Canterbury for adultery with Margaret Tye. (X. 8. 5. 8r). They appeared, purgation (double) septima manu. He did not appear and was declared contumacious. Adjourned. She produced twelve (named) and was monished not to associate with Humphrey, except where by the necessity of life she could not avoid him. (X. 8. 5. 13v). He did not appear. Declared convicted and contumacious.

457 William Bolton miller for adultery with Alice Ducke. (Folkestone, X. 1. 5. 116v, 117r, 126r). She confessed. He said that about three weeks before Christmas she brought to him at his mill a bushel of wheat. While he was away the chickens had scraped away some of it. He said to Alice 'it were a good deed to lay thee down'. She said she would, if I would marry her. He said 'not while I live'. Purgation quarta manu for him. She was to appear again to receive penance. He did not appear: penalty reserved.

458 Alice wife of Thomas Calcote taken in adultery on New Year's Day with Richard Mylls. (St. Mary Northgate, Canterbury, X. 1. 2. 1/2v) Her husband maintains her naughtiness. Marginal note: Excommunicated**** (X. 8. 5. 56v). Purgation septima manu manu. Compugators produced but said they could not depose beyond what they knew. They had heard evil talk. Purgation failed. Excommunicated. 11 August. She appeared. Penance in the accustomed manner next Sunday. 12 November. Absolved and penance ordered on Sunday week at Christ Church Canterbury.

*See Appendix 9.
**i.e. X. 1. 6. as noted above.
***[sic]-apparently undecima
****See footnote on page 48

DISCIPLINING OF PRIVATE LIVES

459 Joan Grigby is suspected of adultery and is an unquiet woman. (Cranbrook, X. 1. 7. 13v,14r). She did not appear and was excommunicated. A letter from Thomas Yale, chancellor of the archbishop, saying that she was excommunicated by the procurement of her husband and for no cause proved against her and desiring the Commissary to refrain from signifying. 11 November 1566. She is absolved (full text). (17r) A further letter and absolution.

460 Andrew Crompe, formerly of Brabourne now of Horton, for adultery with Alice Sprie of Brabourne. (X. 1. 6. 93v, 94r & v) He confessed. To do penance on the two following Sundays in the church of Brabourne. He petitioned for commutation to a money payment. The Judge because of the need of the poor commuted the penance to payment of 6s 8d to John Powell a poor man, 20s to the churchwardens of Horton, 20s to the churchwardens of Brabourne also 40s next Christmas, 13s 4d for rebuilding the tower of St. Paul Canterbury, 6s 8d for the poor of St. Mary Northgate Canterbury, 3s 4d to a poor man John Rychard, 3s 4d to a poor man called father Hyett of St. Mary Magdalen Canterbury, 6s 8d, the rest of the 4 li to be distributed at the direction of the Judge.

INCEST

Wife's daughter

461 John Awgor of Folkestone for incest with his wife's daughter. (X. 8. 5. 45r). He confessed, but as he would not submit to the ordinances of the church, he was excommunicated. He appeared and petitioned for absolution. He was to do penance in the church of Folkestone on the following Sunday and in the public market place there. Penance was certified. Marginal note: The curate to be written to to absolve him. (98r) Appeared. To show cause why he should not be excommunicated.

462 Walter Gothorne of Sittingbourne for incest with his wife's daughter Elizabeth Reymet. (X. 8. 5. 96v). He confessed the offence for ten years. Adjourned. Footnote: He underwent public penance.

Own daughter

463 Richard Downe of Tenterden for incest with his own daughter. (X. 8. 5. 104r, 105v). Did not appear. Excommunicated. Appeared and petitioned absolution but denied the charge. Purgation septima manu at the next General Chapter at Goudhurst and all women who were present at the birth were to be cited to attend. He was monished to produce the woman. He said his daughter came creeping to him one night when he was asleep, but he never had carnally to do with her. Elizabeth alias Isabel Downe did not appear. Excommunicated. (107r). He appeared and voluntarily confessed that his daughter came to bed to him three or four nights after his wife's death. Adjourned to hear the will of the Archbishop. To appear before the Archbishop after the Feast of the Purification. (X. 1. 4. 76v, 77r). She is presented for having a child she admits by her father. 'dying' (?she or the child) Marginal note: Before the Archbishop.

464 Bartholomew Fowle is suspected of incest with his daughter. (Boughton Monchelsea, X. 1. 7. 29v, 30r). He did not appear. Excommunicated. Later he appeared and was absolved. His wife Alice and daughter aged 12 appeared. The daughter admitted her father kissed her, but otherwise denied. He denied he had provoked her by word or deed. His wife said he accused her of being a thief and drove her out of doors like a dog. He had caught his daughter in his arms and kissed her for which she (his wife) felt offended. Ordered to do penance next Sunday in the church of Boughton Monchelsea in the form handed to him. He petitioned for commutation of the penance for a money payment. The Judge directed him to pay 10s to John Maister for the poor of the parish. (42r) Adjourned.

Brother's widow

465 Herbert Moore has begotten his brother Anthony More's widow Marion Moore of Robertsbridge and married her at Lewes. (Sandhurst, X. 1. 2. 1/29v, Y. 2. 24. 50v). He submitted. To do penance at Sandhurst on three following Sundays, reading from a written schedule. Penance certified. Dismissed.

Wife's sister

466 Bartholomew Harrenden for fornication with Winifred Knotts, his wife's sister. (Frittenden, X. 1. 3. 70v, 71r). He confessed and submitted in tears. He is to do penance on the two following Sundays and in the church of Cranbrook on the Sunday after Christmas. Penance was certified. The woman, who has not yet given birth, is at Netherfield in Sussex.

Relationship not given

467 Thomas Barton for incest with Agnes Garton when his servant and now living at Willesborough (Boughton Aluph, X. 1. 5. 101v, 102r). He said that as his servant she slept in the same room as he and his wife. She called out in the night and, when they asked her next day why she did so, she said that somebody lay on her. She told one Fox's wife that it was he. He denied. Purgation quarta manu. Marginal note: Paid (?7)d.

468 Alice Ramyse had a child by her brother-in-law*. (St. Dunstan Canterbury, X. 1. 2. 1/3v). Did not appear. Excommunicated. Later appeared and absolved.

BIGAMY

469 Richard Fawkon is suspected of having two wives. (Cranbrook, X. 1. 4. 92v, 93r). He has left the parish. Citation served. Did not appear. Excommunicated.

*Often at this time a step brother was described as a brother in law.

DISCIPLINING OF PRIVATE LIVES

470   John Ashete has put away his wife and married another. (Upchurch, X. 1. 3. 63v, 64r). The vicar certifies that it appears from examination by the churchwardens that his wife is dead.

471.   William Sharp of St. Mary Northgate Canterbury married Helen Swetman of St. Peter Canterbury and later married Elizabeth Tipping. (Y. 2. 20 39r, 42v, 48v, Y. 2. 24. 2v, 12r). He agreed that he had lived in adultery with Elizabeth Tipping and that he contracted marriage with Helen Swetman, banns published three times two years ago. He then married Elizabeth Tipping in the face of the church. He contracted with Rabege Nash about a fortnight before Christmas but banns were forbidden. The Judge ordered they were not to consort together, except in church or public places. He is to appear at the next sitting to show cause why he should not be excommunicated and to answer a charge of fornication with Margery Cheseman. Later: he was monished to produce Cheseman or a certificate of date and place of her death. Helen Swetman appeared and said she did not want to be in the case or to have the man.

472   Joan Ramesdale of St. Mary Bredin Canterbury, after being married to Ramesdale for twelve years married Hamond Joye. (Y. 2. 20. 42v, 48r, Y. 2. 24, 1v). She said she was married at St. Andrew Canterbury without banns and agreed her first husband was alive. Ickham, the rector, Ramesdale & Joy to be summoned and she is to show cause why she should not be excommunicated. She appeared and was ordered penance. Performance was certified and she was ordered to repeat her penance in the market place in Canterbury on the following Sunday.

473   Henry Stuppyn of Upper Hardres has two wives. (Y. 2. 24. 107v). He married Avice Boughton of Elham twenty years ago and she left him with property of his value 20li. He heard she was drowned in the barge going to London. Later he married Alice Mount of Elham.

474   William Gowlde married Alice Rowe and it is not known if her husband is alive. (Barham, X. 1. 2. 1/12r, Y. 2. 24. 38r). Andrew Long said he met Rowe, husband of Alice Row als Gold in London. Row lives (? with the Earl of Brentford).

475   Robert Maynard of Headcorn has the wife of William Saunder as well as his own. (X. 8. 5. 35v). He appeared and agreed that his wife was the wife of William Saunder who left the parish six years ago and had not been heard of. Monished not to associate with the woman till he had heard of the death of Saunder and to appear again. Later: he did not appear. Excommunicated. The woman appeared, paid fee and was directed to produce a certificate of Saunder's death.

476 William Redesdall has two wives living. (River, X. 1. 7. 126v, 127r). He said he had no certain knowledge of the death of his first wife. He saw her seven or eight weeks ago at Dover and heard she was married again in Flanders. He married his second wife about three years ago. They have lived together all that time, for the last quarter of a year at River. His first wife ran away from him at Canterbury in the year in which Sir Thomas Wyatt rose*. He was monished not to keep company with the woman he has, but to separate. He was to do penance in the church of River next Sunday and in the market place of Dover on the following Sunday and to sit there in the stocks with a paper about his head declaring the cause viz. that he has two wives living.

477 (blank) Harrys has a wife whose husband is alive named Richard, a sawyer. (Faversham, X. 1. 7. 153v, 154r, 155r). Margaret appeared and said her first husband left her about fifteen years ago within a year of their marriage. She has never seen him since and thinks he is dead, though she has heard lately of strangers that he is living. Atkyns of Faversham was in London lately where he saw her husband, Richard Wryght, at one of the quays there. Adjourned.

478 Elizabeth Essex married John Blackhall late curate of Snave who was already married. (Snave, X. 1. 5. 149v). She did not appear. Excommunicated. Later she appeared and agreed she married Blackhall about half a year ago, not knowing he had another wife. After three nights Blackhall left her eleven weeks ago and she had not heard of him since. She is to do penance next Sunday in the church of Shadoxhurst and in her own church of Snave on the Sunday following. Marginal note: absolved without fee.

479 Walter Colton reader of Guston for having two wives. (X. 1. 7. 81v, 82r). He said he had had four wives. The first was Joan Lacy of Preston by Wingham whom he married about 21 years ago. After about ¾ year she died. Then he married Margaret Yorke servant of Mr. Randall of Badlesmere to whom he was married for 6 or 7 years. She died and was buried in the churchyard of St. Mildred Canterbury. The third wife was Joan Fawkell living at Bodiam. They were married at Sandhurst 5 or 6 years ago. He does not know if she is dead or not. His fourth wife was Margaret Rychards widow whom he married at Canterbury about two years ago. He met his brother last harvest, but his brother said nothing of his (Walter's) wife. One Jefferey of Canterbury told him that she was alive at Whitsuntide. He was monished not to keep company with Margaret Rychards any longer and to do the usual penance next Sunday in the church of Guston and to appear for further penance to be given.

* Wyatt's Rebellion 1554.

DISCIPLINING OF PRIVATE LIVES

MISCELLANEOUS

Bawdry

480   The wife of Bartholomew Henley is suspected of bawdry. She is an evil woman from youth, in whose house Alexander Dence and the wife of Stephen Sharp have many times suspiciously been together. (Cranbrook, X. 1. 3. 74v, 75r). Alexander Dence appeared and denied. Purgation quinta manu.

Burning

481   One Hopper was burnt and divers other imprisoned, whose names we know not. (Cranbrook, X. 1. 2. 1/32v)

482   John Pardew was burnt at Canterbury (Elmsted X. 1. 2. 1/23r)

483   Joan Sole was burnt out of the parish (Horton, X. 1. 2. 1/26v)

Wife beating

484   Thomas Frenchebourn of Westwell gagged his wife Ann on a post and beat her. Another time when lying with him she had a nail or bodkin thrust into her head. He kept her from meat and drink. (Y. 2. 24. 130v). He was monished to end dissension with his wife and was to pay 12d in cash or value (?to her) and to pay 12d before he leaves (?for the poor). She is to prove the second allegation. Later he said that in falling out with her six years ago he took her by the chin and gave her two or three blows about the head or face (a long account of his defence seems to be based on his being half asleep on the occasion of which she complained to neighbours that he thrust a nail or bodkin in her). He denied keeping meat and drink from her.

Bells

485   William Hubbard sexton knolled the great bell at the time of thunder. (Benenden, X. 8. 5. 71v). Did not appear. Excommunicated. To do penance in his parish church. Did not appear. Excommunicated. Later appeared, absolved and dismissed.

486   Bells have been stolen and taken to Mr. Lynche's house at Sandwich. (Seasalter, X. 1. 3. 12v)

Unlicensed midwife

487   Agnes Conny for acting as midwife without authority. (St. Mary Northgate, Canterbury, X. 1. 5. 90v, 91r)

Teaching

488   They have a schoolmaster to teach grammar, but which grammar they know not.* (Tenterden, X. 1. 2. 1/35v)

*Presumably with reference to the Queen's Injunction no. 39

Desertion of a servant

489 The brother of Mary Hendley came with a horse and rode away with her, where they know not. (Selling, X. 1. 2. 1/45v). She came from curate Pettyt's house. Joan wife of Thomas Wallbancke said Mary was away from her master Pettyt because her mistress was cruel.

Usury*

490 Gilbert Heron vicar of Elmsted for usury. (X. 8. 5. 1r & v). He agrees that John Bulfinche had 7 li a year of him for 7 years, for which he had 7 li 7s every year. The Judge said he also had from Bulfinch 26s 8d a year for 10 years. Heron said Bulfinch had some land from him. Bulfinch said the land was about 3 acres. Purgation septima manu.

Bonfire revelry

491 Thomas Quidler made a large bonfire. Though warned to leave it, he would not but when the officer was gone, went about the fire with neighbours drinking. On St. Peter's night he made a bigger fire. (Ashford, X. 1. 2. 1/30v). He is to appear to show cause why he should not be punished.

Neglected tombs

492 The places where Margaret Grigesby widow and Margaret daughter of Alexander Grigesby gentleman are buried in the chancel of Loose are unpaved, very noisome and uncomely. Alexander Grigesby is responsible for his daughter and Alexander Dennce of Cranbrook is executor of Margaret Grigesby widow. (Z. 3. 8. 145v, 146r). He did not appear. Excommunicated.

Hospitals

493 A memorandum about the foundation and establishment of the Hospital of St. Lawrence founded by the Abbot of St. Augustine's Monastery. Mention, too, of Harbledown and St. John's (Hospitals). (X. 1. 3. 166v)

Arrest after 40 days

494 Simon Gilbert lately of Old Romney and now of Snargate excommunicate 40 days. (X. 1. 6. 8v). Petitions absolution. To do penance in church next Sunday at Old Romney, the following Sunday at New Romney, the following Sunday at Snargate and the following Sunday at Appledore. (15v). To certify penance. Did not appear. Excommunicated. (25v) Penance certified.

*By 5 & 6 Edw VI, c.20 no person should lend any sum of money for any manner of usury or increase to be received or hoped for, above the sum lent. By 13 Eliz I, c. 8. a maximum of 10% interest was allowed.

DISCIPLINING OF PRIVATE LIVES

495 Robert Boleyne alias Gyllan of Ashford to show cause why application should not be made to the Queen for his arrest. (X. 1. 6. 28r). Judge decreed application should be made.

'Lenocinium'*

496 John Wood of Kingsnorth, late of Great Chart for 'lenocinium'. (X. 8. 5. 47Ar). He admitted it. To do penance in his parish church for three Sundays. Did not appear. Excommunicated. (93v). Penance certified.

Deceiving the Court

497 Margaret Yngland had another child before marriage and made one man do penance for it when another was the father. (Old Romney, X. 1. 5. 54v, 55r). She admitted the child and was ordered to appear at the General Chapter to receive penance. Testimonial from William Jompe. (55v, 56r). She denied causing the wrong man to do penance and was monished.

Respect for elders and betters

498 Joan Ynglishe servant to Sir Robert Pyborn uses her tongue inordinately toward her elders and betters (Mongeham, X. 1. 7. 174v, 175r). She has been with Pyborne about 10 years. She said that John Burton called her uncle Sir Robert Pyborn thief and dog and said that Loo of Canterbury was Mr. Fisher's bastard and that the said Loo was indebted more than he was worth. She then said that Burton lied. To do penance on the following Sunday in the church of Gt. Mongeham without linen vestment, but she will hold a white rod.

---

*Pandering or pimping, professing to be a bawd (Lewis & Short's Latin Dictionary).

CHURCH LIFE IN KENT

A page of a liber cleri
(Transcript of the facing plate)

Smarden billa	Rector Ic(ono)mi Paroch(ian)i	Mr. Gregor(y) Dode Laurenc(ius) Wolf Antony Redar Jacobus Lake Thomas Norton Joh(an)n(es) (Scherpe*sen)	 iur(atus) no(n comparuit) Jur(ati) no(n comparuit)
Tenterden billa	Vicarius Cur(atus) Ic(ono)mi Paroch(ian)i	nullus D(omin)us Johannes Ropson W(illia)m(us) Hoball W(illia)m(us) Leedes Stephanus Cowper Thomas Stace Thomas Austen Ric(ardus) Allen	 jur(atus) no(n comparuit) no(n comparuit) iur(atus) no(n comparuit) egr(otat) no(n comparuit)
Hothefeld billa r exh(ibita) per Tho- (mam) Bull	Rector Cur(atus) Ic(ono)mi Paroch(ian)i	Mag(iste)r Henricus Goodrick nullus Thomas Bull Rob(er)t(us) Wanderton Nicolaus Topley Henricus Turner Laurentius Howsoley	comp(aruit) per me ** Jur(ati) ?iur(atus) no(n comparuit) iur(atus)
Hawkeherst billa	Vicar(ius) Curat(us) Ic(ono)mi Paroch(ian)i	D(omin)us Hugo Trevor Tho(mas) Mercer Jo Goodman Edward(us) Dunck Richard(us) Alkyn Georgius Afford	 h(ab)et ad exhibend (um) fucultates sibi concessas a collegio &c. (die Ven- eris a festo Epiphane Jur(ati) Jur(ati)
Boughton Malherbe	Rector Ic(ono)mi Paroch(ian)i.	Mag(iste)r Thomas Langley Johannes Genyngs Johannes Gorh(am)	co(m)par(uit) Jur(ati)

* Though the 'r' is badly written here, his name appears elsewhere as SHARPP or SHAPP (Z.3.5. 150r) or SHERPE (Z.3.7 61r)

** The Registrar or his clerk evidently acted as his proctor for appearance.

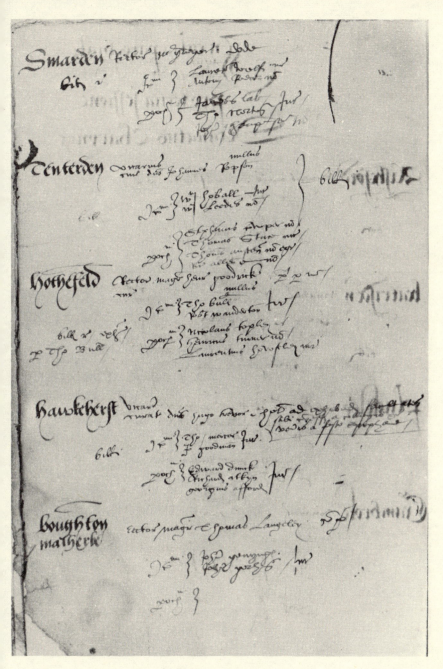

A page of liber cleri

As some of the writing on reverse side of the original page shows through, a magnifying glass will be found useful in deciphering.

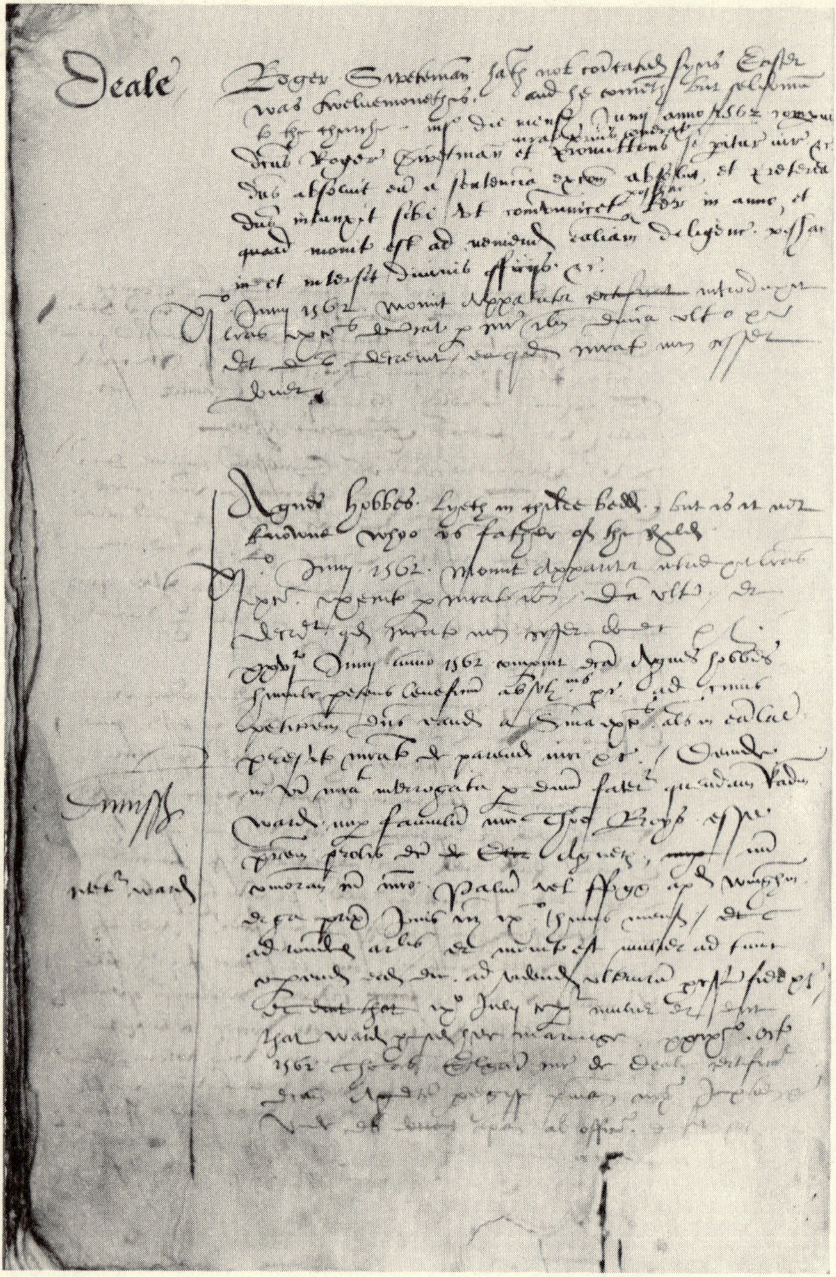
Deale

A page of detecta with the action taken on them

DISCIPLINING OF PRIVATE LIVES

A PAGE OF DETECTA WITH THE ACTION TAKEN ON THEM.

Deale

    Roger Sweteman hath not co(mmuni)cated syns Easter was twelve-monethes and he cometh but seldome to the churche*. iiij^{o}die mens (is) Junij anno 1562 comparuit d(i)c(t)us Roger Swetman et iura-(mento) prius onera(tus) promittens se pariturum iur(i) &c. d(omin)us absolvit eum a sentencia excom(municationis) absolvit**, et preterea d(omin)us iniunxit sibi***ut com(m)unicet posthac ter in anno, et quoad monit(us) est ad veniend(um) eccl(es)iam diligenc(ia) pos(t)hac et intersit divinis officiis &c.

xj^o Junii 1562 Mount apparitor introduxit l(ite)ras exco(mmunicationis) de(clar)at(as) per cur(atum) ib(ide)m d(omin)ica ultima &c. et d(ominu)s decrevit q(uo)d curat(us) non cesset donec...

    Agnes Hobbes lyeth in childe bedd, but is it not knowne whoo is father of the child.

xj^o Junij 1562 Mount apparitor introduxit l(ite)ras exco(mmunicationis) execut(as) per curat(um) ibi d(ominic)a ult(ima). Dominus decrevit quod curatus non cesset donec ...

xxvj^{o}Junii anno 1562 comp(ar)uit d(ic)ta Agnes Hobbes humil(ite)r petens beneficium absol(ution)is &c. ad cuius peticionem d(omin)us eand-(em) a S(ente)n(c)ia exco(mmunicationi)s als in ea(m) lata, prestito iura(men)to ad parend(um) iuri &c.

(Marginal notes: 'dimissa' 'citetur Ward'). Deinde **** in vi iura(men)-ti interrogata per d(omin)um fatet(u)r quendam Rad(olphu)m Ward nuper famulu(m) m(agist)ri Tho(me) Boys esse p(at)rem prolis d(ic)te Agnetis, nu(nc) com(m)oran(tem) cu(m) m(agist)ro Pa]m(er) vel Fogg ap(u)d Wingham erga prox(imum) (diem) Jovis viz. ix^o huius mensis. (Citetur Ward) ad r(esp)ond(en)dum ar(ticu)lis et monit(a) est mulier ad tunc co(m)parend(um) eod(em) die ad videndum ultemum processum fieri &c.

ix^{o}Julij co(m)par(ui)t mulier et dic(i)t that Ward promised her marriage.
xxix Oct(obris) 1562 Thomas Elgar curatus de Deale certifica(vi)t d(ict)am Agnete(m) peregisse p(e)n(itenti)am iux(ta) in(iun)x(io)nem &c. unde d(ominu)s decrevit ipsam ab offic(io)desit.

---

*The end of the prewritten entry can be seen from the change in the handwriting. The new date is also a guide, though dates are not always given

**The word 'absolvit' seems to have been written twice by mistake.

***Presumably more correctly 'ei'. Grammar is not always of the best.

****Presumably on a later date not given, as there is mention of the 9th of the same month.

A TRANSLATION OF THE LATIN PORTION OF THE ITEMS ON PLATE 2

3 June 1562. The said Roger Swetman appeared and, being first sworn and promising to obey law, the Judge absolved him from the sentence of excommunication and further the Judge enjoined him to communicate in future three times a year and monished him to go to church diligently in future and attend Divine Service &c.

11 June 1562. Mount the apparitor introduced letters of excommunication published by the curate there last Sunday and the Judge decreed that the curate should not relax in the matter until (the sentence is unfinished*

---

11 June 1562. Mount the apparitor introduced letters of excommunication published by the curate there last Sunday and the Judge decreed that the curate should not relax in the matter until (the sentence is unfinished).*

Dismissed Ward to be cited

26 June 1562. The said Agnes Hobbes appeared and humbly petitioned for the benefit of absolution &c. on whose petition the Judge absolved her from the sentence of excommunication, first taking her oath to obey the law, &c. Then on the strength of her oath, being questioned by the Judge, she confessed that a certain Ralph Ward, recently servant of Mr. Thomas Boys, was father of her child, saying that he was staying with Mr. Palmer alias Fogg at Wingham till next Thursday, 9th of this month. (Ward is to be cited) to answer articles and the woman was monished to appear on the same day to see the last stage of the cause.

9 July. The woman appeared and said that Ward promised her marriage.

29 October 1562. Thomas Elgar curate of Deal certified that the said Agnes had performed her penance according to the injunction, whereupon the Judge decreed that she was free of the cause.**

---

*No doubt something like 'further advice is received from the Judge' is intended.

**The last line of the original is faint and difficult to decipher. The word transcribed 'decrevit' may be something else, as the last word is also evidently a verb, where one would expect 'dimissam' or 'dimitti', but this, even abbreviated, would have a double s or t. If this sentence had been longer, one would suspect that the writer had forgotten the construction by the time he reached the end, but that would hardly seem to be the case with such a short sentence.

APPENDIX 1

VOLUMES USED FOR THIS BOOK

These volumes are contemporary manuscript records deposited in Canterbury Cathedral Library and are described by their Library reference.

The terms Visitation and General Chapter below refer to the libri cleri.*

All dates are for the year ending on March 24th.

Archdeacon's Court
___

X. 1. 2. (part 1)	Detecta 1560
X. 1. 3.	" 1561
X. 8. 5.	Act Book 1559-1563
X. 1. 4.	Detecta 1562
X. 1. 5.	" 1563-4
	Visitations 1563, 1564
X. 1. 6.	Act Book 1564-5
X. 1. 7.	Detecta 1565
Z. 3. 5.	Visitation 1559
	General Chapter 1560
Z. 3. 7.	Visitations 1560, 1561, 1562
	General Chapter 1561, 1562

Consistory Court
___

Y. 2. 20 (ff. 41-49)	Draft detecta 1559
Y. 2. 24	Act Book 1559-1564
Z. 3. 8. (Exempt parishes)	Detecta 1561-1563, 1565
	Visitations 1561, 1562
	General Chapters 1560, 1565
X. 8. 2. (Exempt parishes)	Detecta 1564
	Visitation 1564

*See page 3, second paragraph.

APPENDIX 2

HEADING OF THE QUEEN'S INJUNCTIONS OF 1559

Extracted from the full text published in 'Visitation Articles and Injunctions' by W.H. Frere (Alcuin Club Collections, vol. XVI, p.8).

1. Abolishing foreign authority.
2. Images.
3. Monthly sermons for works of faith. No pilgrimages, candles or praying on beads.
4. Quarterly sermons.
5. Lord's Prayer, Creed and Commandments to be recited in English.
6. Provision of the Bible and Paraphrase of Erasmus.
7. Haunting alehouses by ecclesiastical persons.
8. Unlicensed preachers.
9. Letters of the Word and fautors of usurped power.
10. Keeping of parish register.
11. Distribution of fortieth part of revenues of benefice by non-resident incumbents.
12. Exhibitions for scholars.
13. Fifth part of benefice to be allocated for repairs.
14. These Injunctions to be read once a quarter.
15. Payment of tithes.
16. Clergy to have their own copy of the New Testament and Paraphrase
17. Clergy to be ready to comfort the sick.
18
19. Processions and perambulations. The Litany.
20. Keeping of holy day.
21. Reconciliation of those contending with their neighbours.
22. Maintenance of the ceremonies of the Church.
23. Abolition of things superstitious.
24. Provision of a pulpit.
25. Provision of a poor chest and distribution of alms.
26. Simony.
27. Reading of homilies.
28. Refraining from abuse of priests and ministers.
29. Marriage of clergy.
30. Apparel of ministers.
31. Heresies.
32. Sorcery, witchcraft etc.
33. Attendance at own parish church only
34. Victualling in time of Divine Service.
35. Images etc. forbidden in houses.
36. Disturbance of preachers.
37. Rash talking of Scripture.
38. People to give quiet attendance to Services.
39. Grammar of Henry VIII to be taught by schoolmasters.
40-42 Teachers to be licensed and teach reverence of God's true religion and learn sentences of Scripture inducing to godliness.

APPENDIX 2

43. Appointment of unlearned priests.
44. Teaching of catechism.
45. Information for the Queen's Visitors.
46. Overseers in every parish to see people go to church.
47. Inventories of church goods for the Queen's Visitors.
48. Litany on Wednesdays and Fridays.
49. Continuance of singing in church.
50. Against slanderous and infamous words.
51. Against heretical and seditious books.
52. Reverence at prayer.
53. Curates to read distinctly.

Then follow some instructions unnumbered:-
    The meaning of oaths of allegiance.
    Altars and Communion tables.
    Sacramental bread.
    Directions for prayer.

APPENDIX 3

ANALYSIS OF CLERGY 1559-61
(Vols. Z.3.5., Z.3.7., Z.3.8)

An analysis has been made of the clergy recorded in the Visitations of 1559 and 1560 (excluding exempt parishes) and 1561 with this result:-

	1559	1560	1561	1561 (exempt parishes)
Rectors named	67	74	82	20(2 are Priors)
" vacant	29	19	14	1
Vicars named	57	65	76	14
" vacant	35	24	16	3
Curates in charge named	9	15	15	10
" " " vacant	20	13	14	1
*Assistant curates	46	32	41	11
	263	242	258	60
Readers	-	23	31	9
	263	265	289	69

The totals do not represent separate persons, as, apart from incumbencies held in plurality, a rector or vicar might act as curate of another parish and a curate might serve more than one parish. The analysis of the exempt parishes is incomplete, because the records of the deaneries of Sittingbourne and Charing are wanting and in that of the deanery of Canterbury the names of clergy have in many cases not been given. Nevertheless, the figures make it clear that vacant livings were being filled, though there was no inflow of additional clergy. The establishment of readers no doubt relieved many curates, enabling them to be promoted to benefices.

---

*These may be temporarily in charge, where the incumbency is marked as vacant. The preceding two items of curates are for parishes which have no space provided in the record for a rector or vicar, so they were presumably in charge.

APPENDIX 4

DIRECTIONS TO THE CLERGY (1561)
(Vol. Z. 3. 7. fol 41v)

1. Diligently to instruct the youth of their parish in the catechism and to certify how the youth have and do resort to the church to be instructed.

2. Diligently to see that the register in their church is well kept and that with great circumspection. Every curate is to make a particular certificate on whole sheets of paper of all the names of those who have been buried, christened and wedded from a year last Easter to the present time. The lists to be produced at Canterbury on the Wednesday after Trinity Sunday or before. They are to show how many that were dead were householders.

3. Every curate is at the same time to certify the names of all who did not receive Communion at Easter last and how many have not received thrice in accordance with the Injunction.

4. Every curate within his own parish diligently to enquire if any person, man or woman, has any dead man's or dead woman's goods in their hands kept without authority from the Ordinary and to produce a list of their names.

5. Curates are to admonish their churchwardens & parishioners, on pain of the law, to purge and cleanse their parish church of all monuments of superstition or idolatry before Whit Sunday and the curates are to certify accordingly on Whit Tuesday next.

6. All sequestrators of benfices are to appear at St. Margaret Canterbury on the Wednesday after Trinity Sunday producing an account in writing of their sequestrations and bringing with them the letters of sequestration.

7. Curates & churchwardens of every parish diligently to search among their parishioners that they use no primers or other book of prayers in Latin not authorised or allowed by the Queen.

8. Curates are to use one uniformity both in Divine Service and in administration of the Sacrament, as has already been prescribed to them.

9. Every curate between now and the next Visitation is to learn 'without book' either in Latin or in English chapter 6 of Baruch, chapter 6 of St. John's Gospel, chapter 16 of St. Matthew's Gospel, chapter 11 of 1 Corithians and chapter 18 of Revelation.*
Marginal addition: Item that they choose a Dean.

---

*This list ends with an exclamation mark in contemporary hand. The clerk was evidently impressed. He repeats the chapters in tabulated form in the bottom margin.

APPENDIX 5

ANALYSIS OF DETECTA 1559-60
(Vol. X.1.2)

The analysis represents offences, not individuals. Where the offence is a joint one, e.g. fornication, irregular marriage, etc., it counts as one, but where several individuals are charged with the same offence in one presentment, e.g. a group not receiving Communion, each is treated as a separate offender.

The analysis of offences is as follows:-

The Clergy

1. No clergy — 29
2. Not resident — 36
3. Has another benefice — 27
4. Failure to teach (Catechism, Lord's Prayer or to prepare for Communion) — 6
5. Lack of sermons — 8
6. Irregularity of sermons — 12
7. Failure in duty — 8
8. Gaming or frequenting ale houses — 4
9. Other misdeameanours (leaving benefice, appointing reader irregularly, not relieving the poor) — 3

The Church

10. Chancel in decay — 32
11. Church in decay — 19
12. Parsonage in decay — 25
13. Churchyard or its fencing in decay — 8
14. Rood loft not removed — 7
15. Furnishings or ornaments lacking or irregular — 7
16. Bible or Service books lacking — 15
17. Paraphrase of Erasmus lacking — 19
18. Popery and reaction from it — 10
19. Patrons of living named — 11

APPENDIX 5

Laymen and the Church

20. Failure to attend parish church — 33
21. Failure to take Communion (or doing so when not in charity) — 32
22. Victualling or bowling in time of Divine Service — 10
23. Popery — 8
24. Witholding church funds, cattle, sheep etc. — 89

Private Lives of Laymen

25. Scold, teller of tales abuser, railer, swearer, brawler or drunkard — 38
26. Husband and wife living apart — 13
27. Suspected immorality — 17
28. Fornication or bastardy — 39
29. Adultery — 13
30. Irregular marriages — 4
31. Suspected bigamy — 2
32. Buggery — 1
33. Suspected witchcraft — 18
34. Neglect of duty by church officers — 9
35. Failure in duty of executors — 7
36. Harbouring a suspected woman or one with child — 8
37. Slander — 1

Miscellaneous

38.	Wearing beads	1
39.	Concealing a suspected person	1
40.	Efficiency of a schoolmaster	1
41.	Burning (?heretics)	3
42.	"Suspected with a poynter'*	1
43.	Marriage or baptism out of the parish	4
44.	Absence from the choir	1
45.	Suspected incest	1
46.	Failure to give to the poor	5

---

*The meaning is uncertain. It is of a woman and it may refer to suspicion of association with a man named Poynter.

APPENDIX 6

VISITATION ARTICLES FOR EXEMPT PARISHES. 1564
(X. 8. 2. fol. 28r)

Articles ministered to the Churchwardens and Sidemen of the Churches and Chapels exempt in the Visitation of the said exempts kept by Mr. Vincent Denne Commissary General of the diocese of Canterbury in the year of Our Lord God 1564.

---

1. Whether you have a minister resident amongst you in your parish attending to his duty and, if not, in whose default the lack is.

2. Whether there be any of your parishioners old or young that do not frequent the church on Sundays and holy days as Christian men ought to do.

3. Whether there be any that have not received the holy Sacrament of the Body and Blood of our Saviour Christ at Easter last or other convenient times.

4. Whether there be any that walk, talk or sleep in time of Divine Service or sermon.

5. Whether there be any fornicators of adulterers or any vehemently suspected for the same, or any bawds, receivers or counsellors of such lewd persons.

6. Whether there be any notorious drunkards, great swearers or common scolds and disquieters of their neighbours.

10. (sic) Whether your perambulations were used of late according to the Queen's Majesty's Injunctions and to the intent and meaning of the same and not superstitiously abused as it has been.

11. (sic) Whether you have any other excess, enormity or default contrary to God's Word, the Queen's Majesty's ecclesiastical laws and Injunctions or any other civil ordinance made by your Ordinary.

APPENDIX 7

SOME EXTRACTS FROM CONTEMPORARY STATUTES

These extracts are taken from the folio edition of 'Statutes of the Realm' volumes 3 and 4 (1817-19). The section numbers of an Act seem to be a matter for editors and may differ from those in other editions. They were evidently not in the original Acts.

Spelling has been modernised and parts superfluous for this purpose have been omitted.

Non-residence
21 Hy VIII, c.13

15. Every spiritual person, beneficed with any parsonage or vicarage, shall be personally resident and abiding in at and upon his said benefice, or at any one of them at the least; and in case he shall absent himself wilfully by the space of two months to be at several times in one year, he shall forfeit for every such default 10 li, half to the king and half to the party that will sue for the same in any of the king's courts.
(A number of exceptions are made for those overseas, going on a pilgrimage, studying at a university, personal resident chaplains, etc.)

Popery
3 & 4 Edw VI, C. 10

1. All books* called antiphoners, missals, grailes, processionals, manuals, legends, pies, portyses, primers in latin or english, couchers, journals, ordinals or other books or writings whatsoever heretofore used for the service of the church, written or printed in the english or latin tongue, other than such as shall be set forth by the king's majesty, shall be clearly and utterly abolished, extinguished and forbidden for ever to be used or kept in this realm or elsewhere in the king's dominions.

2. Images in churches of stone, timber, alabaster or earth, graven, carved or painted, shall be defaced and destroyed.

---

*Antiphoner, the choir book.
Missal the book of the mass.
Graile (gradale), the choir book for high mass.
Manual, contained procedure for administration of the sacrament etc.
Legend, the book containing the lessons to be read.
Pie or portuis ordered the manner of performing Divine Service.

APPENDIX 7

6. This is not to extend to any image or picture set or graven upon any tomb in any church, chapel or churchyard, only* for a monument of any king, prince, nobleman or other dead person, which hath not been commonly reputed or taken for a saint.

Eating of meat at fasting times

2 & 3 Edw VI c.19

1. No person shall willingly and wittingly eat any manner of flesh upon any friday or saturday or the embring days, or in lent, nor at any other day commonly reputed as a fish day, on pain of forfeiting 10s and imprisonment for 10 days.

3. Provided that this statute shall not extend to any person that hath obtained any licence of the king; nor to any person being of great age and in debility or weakness thereby; nor to any person being sick or notably hurt, without fraud or covin, during the time of his sickness; nor to any woman being with child or lying in child bed for eating of such one kind of flesh as she shall have great lust unto, neither to any such as heretofore have obtained any licence in due form of the archbishop of Canterbury.

4. And all archbishops, bishops, archdeacons and their officers shall have power to inquire of offenders in the premises....

5 Eliz I, c.5.

11. Wednesdays shall also be fish days

12. For the maintenance of the navy, and for the sparing and increase of flesh victual, it shall not be lawful to any person to eat any flesh upon any days now usually observed as fish days.

13. Provided that all persons which by reason of notorious sickness shall be enforced for recovery of health to eat flesh for the time of their sickness shall be sufficiently licensed by the bishop of the diocese, or by the parson vicar or curate of the parish where such person shall be sick, which licence shall be made in writing and signed by such bishop, parson, vicar or curate and not endure longer than the time of the sickness...

---

*i.e. solely.

CHURCH LIFE IN KENT

Disturbing preachers etc. 1 Mary ss. 2, c.3.	If any person or persons of their own power and authority do or shall, willingly and of purpose by open and overt word, fact, act, or deed, maliciously or contemptuously molest, let 'disturb, vex or trouble, disquiet or misuse any preacher licensed, allowed or authorised to preach, or any parson, vicar, parish priest or curate or any lawful priest preparing, saying, doing, singing, ministering or celebrating the mass or other such Divine Service, or pull down, deface, spoil, abuse, break or otherwise unreverently handle or order the Sacrament of the Altar, or the pyx or canapy wherein the said Sacrament is or shall be, or any altar or altars or any crucifix or cross, then such offender, his aider, procurer or abettor, shall be apprehended by any constable or churchwarden of the parish and brought to a Justice of the Peace and he upon due accusation thereupon had and made shall commit the said person to safe keeping and custody. And within six days the said Justice with one other Justice shall diligently examine the offence aforesaid and if the two said Justices find the accused guilty of the said offence they shall commit the said person to the gaol by the space of three months and to the next Quarter Sessions after the end of the three months. At which Quarter Sessions on his reconciliation and repentance he shall be discharged upon sufficient surety of his good bearing and behaviour. And if he will not be reconciled and repent he shall be further committed to gaol by the said Justices until he shall be reconciled and be penitent.
Brawling or fighting in church precincts 5 & 6 Edw VI, C.4.	1. If any person shall by words only quarrel chide or brawl, in any church or churchyard, it shall be lawful to the ordinary of the place, where the same offence shall be done, and proved by two lawful witnesses, to suspend any person so offending; if he be a layman from entrance of the church and if he be a clerk, from the ministration of his office, for so long a time as the said ordinary shall think meet according to the fault. 2. If any person shall smite or lay any violent hands upon another, in any church of churchyard, then ipso facto every person so offending shall be deemed excommunicate, and be excluded from the fellowship and company of Christ's congregation.

78

APPENDIX 7

	3.	If any person shall maliciously strike any person with any weapon, in any church or churchyard; or shall draw any weapon in church or churchyard, to the intent to strike another with the same weapon; he shall, on conviction by verdict of twelve men, or by his own confession, or by two lawful witnesses, at the assizes or sessions, be adjudged to have one of his ears cut off; and if he have no ears, he shall be burned in the cheek with a hot iron, having the letter F, whereby he may be known and taken for a fray-maker and fighter: and besided he shall be and stand ipso facto excommunicated as aforesaid.
Use of Book of Common Prayer 1 Eliz I, c.2.	2.	All ministers in any cathedral or parish church or other place, shall be bounden to say and use the mattens, evensong, celebration of the Lord's Supper, and administration of each of the sacraments, and all the common and open prayer, in such order and form as is mentioned in the book authorized by parliament in the 5 & 6 Edw VI with one alteration or addition of certain lessons to be used on every Sunday in the year, and the form of the litany altered and corrected*, and two sentences only added in the delivery of the sacrament to the communicants, and none other or otherwise.
Attendance at church 1 Eliz I, c. 2.	3.	Every person shall diligently and faithfully, having no lawful or reasonable excuse to be absent, endeavour themselves to resort to their parish church or chapel accustomed, or, upon reasonable let thereof, to some usual place where common prayer and such service of god shall be used in such time of let, upon every Sunday and other days ordained and used to be kept as holidays, and then and there to abide orderly and soberly, during the time of common prayer, preaching, or other service of god there to be used and ministered; on pain that every person so offending shall forfeit for every such offence 12d, to be levied by the churchwardens of the parish where such offence shall be done, to the use of the poor of the same parish, of the goods lands and tenements of such offender, by way of distress.

---

*i.e. omitting 'from the tyrrany of the bishop of Rome and all his detestable enormities'

Ornaments of the church. 1 Eliz I, c.2.	13.	Such ornaments of the church, and of the ministers thereof, shall be retained and used, as was in the Church of England by authority of parliament in the second year of the reign of king Edward the sixth, until other order shall be therein taken by the authority of the queen's majesty, with the advice of her commissioners appointed and authorized under the great seal of England for causes ecclesiastical, or of the metropolitan of this realm.
Witchcraft 5 Eliz I, c.16	1.	If any person practise or exercise any invocations or conjurations of evil and wicked spirits to or for any intent or purpose; or practise or exercise any witchcraft, enchantment charm or sorcery, whereby any person shall happen to be killed or destroyed, every such offender, their counsellors and aiders being convicted shall suffer pains of death as a felon and shall lose the benefit of sanctuary and clergy....
	2.	If any person shall use, practise or exercise witchcraft, enchantment, charm or sorcery whereby any person shall happen to be wasted, consumed or lamed in his or her body or member, or whereby any goods or chattels of any person shall be destroyed, wasted or impaired, then every such offender, his counsellors and aiders shall for his first offence suffer imprisonment by the space of one whole year and once in every quarter of the said year shall in some market town upon the market day stand openly upon the pillory by the space of six hours and there shall openly confess his or her error and offence, and for the second offence shall suffer death as a felon.

A further section adds the same penalty as section 2 for first offence of any person taking upon him to tell or declare in what place any treasure might be found. For a second such offence the penalty is imprisonment for life and forfeiture of all goods and chattels.

APPENDIX 8

SOME RUBRICS OF THE BOOK OF COMMON PRAYER OF EDWARD VI (1552)
(the Prayer Book referred to in 1 Eliz I C.2 - see page 79)

Wearing of Surplice	And here is to be noted that the minister at the time of the Communion and all other times in his ministration shall use neither alb, vestment nor cope: but, being archbishop or bishop, he shall have and wear a rochet; and, being a priest or deacon, he shall have and wear a surplice only. ('Morning Prayer')
Curate to instruct in Catechism	The Curate of every parish, or some other at his appointment, shall diligently on Sundays and holy days, half an hour before Evensong, openly in the church instruct and examine so many children of his parish sent unto him, as the time will serve and as he shall think convenient, in some part of the Catechism. ('The Confirmation Service')
Parents and masters to send their children for instruction in the Catechism	And all fathers, mothers, masters and dames shall cause their children, servants and apprentices (which have not learnt their Catechism) to come to the church at the time appointed, and obediently to hear and be ordered by the Curate, until such time as they have learned all that is here appointed for them to learn. ('The Confirmation Service')
Evil livers not to receive Communion	If any be an open and notorious evil liver, so that the congregation by him is offended, or have done any wrong to his neighbour by word or deed, the Curate, having knowledge thereof shall call him and advertise him in any wise not to presume to the Lord's Table, until he have openly declared himself to have truly repented and amended his former naughty life, that the congregation may thereby be satisfied which afore were offended: and that he have recompensed the parties whom he hath done wrong unto, or at the least declare himself to be in full purpose so to do as soon as he conveniently may. (' The Communion Service')
Malice and hatred to be reconciled before receiving Communion	The same order shall the Curate use with those betwixt whom he perceiveth malice and hatred to reign, not suffering them to be partakers of the Lord's Table until he know them to be reconciled. ('The Communion Service')

Communion bread   And to take away the superstition which any person hath or might have in the bread and wine, it shall suffice that the bread be such as is usual to be eaten at the table with other meats, but the best and purest wheat bread that conveniently may be gotten. ('The Communion Service')

Attendance at Communion   And note that every parishioner shall communicate at the least three times in the year, of which Easter to be one. ('The Communion Service')

APPENDIX 9

A SENTENCE OF EXCOMMUNICATION
(X. 1. 6. 88r)

In Dei nomine Amen. Nos Vincentius Denne in legibus baccalaureus Reverendi domini Archidiaconi Cantuarie officialis legitime deputatus in quadam causa correctionis ex officio nostro mero contra Georgium Nynne parochie de Thanington mota, rite et legitime procedens eundem Georgium Nunne, eo quod, cum ei detulimus juramentum corporale ad respondendum certis articulis publica voce et fama que dependitur de crimine adulterii sive fornicacionis commisso inter ipsum Georgium et quendam Agnetem Wytherden, uxorem Williami Wytherden de Harbledown, concernentibus, illud idem juramentum ipse subire recusavit et recessit, pronunciamus ipsum contumacem ac in pena sue huiusmodi contumacie manifeste ex officio nostro mero excommunicamus in his scriptis.

        Per me Vincentius Denne.

Lecta fuit & c. per eundem dominum officialem ultimo Octobris ao. 1564 in ecclesia parochiali dive Margarete Cantuarie &c.

In the name of God Amen. We Vincent Denne LL.B. offical of the Reverend the Archdeacon of Canterbury duly appointed rightly and duly proceeding in a certain cause of correction of our own motion against George Nunne of the parish of Thanington, because, when we offered him the corporal oath to answer certain articles arising from public report concerning a case before us of adultery or fornication committed by the said George and a certain Agnes Wytherden, wife of William Wytherden of Harbledown, he refused to take the oath and withdrew, we therefore pronounce him contumacious and as penalty for his said manifest contumacy we by this writing of our own personal authority excommunicate the said George Nynne.

        By me, Vincent Denne.

Read by the said offical on the last day of October 1565 in the parish church of St. Margaret Canterbury

INDEX OF SURNAMES

References in medium type are to item numbers, those in italics are to pages.

ABBEY 136
AFFORD *64*
AGER 115
ALDRETT 335
ALKYN *64*
ALLEN (-YN) 165, 260, *64*
AMOUNTE - see MOUNT
AMYS 166, 331
ANDROW 378
ANTHONY 440
APPRICE 340
APTHOMAS 406
ARROWSMYTHE 180
ASHDAY 392
ASHETE 470
ASKEW 65
ASTONE 373
ATKYNS 477
ATKYNSON 372
AUSTEN (AWSTEN) 399, 434, *64*
AWGOR (OGAR) 454, 561
AYER 160
AYNSTONE 228

BACHLER 342
BAKER 46, 186, 187, 271, 317, 454
BAKESTER 411
BALDEN 178, 278, 375
BALKAM 35
BARGRAVE 431
BARHAM 238
BARLEY 177
BARNARD(E) 393, 414
BARNET 422
BARTLET 349
BARTON 84, 467
BATHERST 434
BAYLY(E) 259, 297
BEARDE 430
BECHER 385
BELKE 231
BELL 254
BELVILO 211
BENSHKYN 276
BENT 431
BINGHAM 5, 139
BISSHOPE 230
BLACKBOURNE 371
BLACKE 239
BLACKHALL 66, 478

BLAKE 354, 433
BLANDE 303
BLECHINDEN 282
BLOCK 381, 382
BOLEYNE 495
BOLTON 457
BONNE — see BOWNE
BONNER (late Bp of London) 376
BOREMAN 326
BOROWE 309
BOUGHTON 473
BOWMAN 337
BOWNE (BONNE) 448
BOYS *65, 66*
BRAKINBURGE (-BURY) 227, 256
BRAYNE 333, 334
BRETT 48
BRIGGS (BRYGS) 429
BROKE 245
BROWNE 36, 356
BRYGS - see BRIGGS
BRYKENDEN 241
BRYSTO 237
BULFINCHE 490
BULL 314, 375, *64*
BURN (Ecclesiastical Law) *5*
BURNELL 130
BUS(S)HE 185, 329
BUTLER 382
BUTTS 427

CAGE 215
CALCOTE 458
CALDHAM 276
CANTERBURY Archbp *1, 8*, 95, 96, 105, 134, 138, 140, 173, 255, 294, 371, 390, 434, 451, 459
Archdeacon *1, 2, 3, 4*, 141, 294
CARIOR 14
CARPENTER 285, 353
CHALBORNE 389
CHAMBERS 171
CHANDLER 444
CHAPMAN 313
CHESEMAN 471
CHEYNEY 445
CHURCH 244
CLARKE 13, 84, 306, 368, 370
CLEYGATE 338

COBB 200
COCKLING 291
COGGER 201
COLE 289
COLLARDE 182
COLLENS 26, 135, 137, 387
COLMAN 261
COLTON 479
COLWELL 222, 231
COMES 429
CONNY 487
CONSANT 192
COPPIN 436
CORNELYS 416
CORTHOPP (CORTOPE) 155, 432
CORTYS 389
COSEN 255
COWPER 377, *64*
CRAFTHORNE 445
CRANMER Archbp 4
CRAYFORD 394
CREWSE 433
CROMPE 460
CUDEN 269
CURLYNGE 275

DALHAM 318
DANYELL 288
DARKNALL 434
DASHE 197
DAVE 423
DAVYE 184
DAWBER 49
DAYE 268
DEACON 71, 352
DEALE 170
DEN(N)CE 240, 345, 480, 492
DENNE *3, 75, 83*
DEWAR 449, 450
DIXON 384
DODD(S) (DODE) 7, 208, *64*
DOWNE 463
DREY 317
DRUETT 348
DUCKE 457
DUNCK *64*
DUNSLAKE 62
DUSTON 362

ELETT 385
ELGAR (-OR) 58, *65, 66*
ELLIS 223
ERASMUS *18*, 131
ESSEX 478

FAWKELL 479
FAWKNER 417
FAWKON 469

FELD 163
FISHCOCKS 402
FISHER (FY-) 322, 498
FLETCHER 183, 345, 357
FOGG *65, 66*
FO(O)RD (FOWRDE) 187, 294, 360
FOULE (FOWLE) 277, 417, 464
FOWLER 162
FOWRDE - see FORD
FRANCKLYSHE 204
FRANKLIN 230
FREMLYN 303
FRENCHE 419
FRENCHAM 332
FRENCHBOURN 484
FREND 443
FROST 384
FULLER 69, 82, 368
FYNCH 367

GADDER 176
GANNTE 302
GARTON 467
GASKOYN 456
GEFFR(E)Y(E) (JEFFEREY) 247, 298, 364, 479
GENYNGS *64*
GERMAN 227
GIBBES 307
GILBERT 282, 287, 494
GODDING 397
GODFREY 244
GOLD (GOWLDE) 474
GOODMAN *64*
GOODRICK *64*
GOODYN 181
GOORN 168
GORE 332
GORHAM 159, *64*
GOSFRITHE 418
GOTELEY 189
GOTHORNE 462
GRENE 194, 412
GRENELL 209
GRENESTED 284
GRENEWAY 421, 422
GRENFELD 423
GRIG(ES)BY(E) 207, 459, 492
GROVE 164
GYLL 196
GYLLAN 495

HAFFENDEN 336
HAKE 363
HALE 446
HALL 378
HALMAN (and see HOLMAN) 16, 51

HANCOCKE 428
HANNYNGE 263
HARDWYN 331
HARENDEN - see HARYNDEN
HARNET 296, 373
HARPE(R) 300, 323
HARP(E)SFELD(E) 141, 294, 305
HARRISON (-YSON) 282, 349
HARRYETT 186
HARRYS 477
HARYNDEN (HARENDEN) 161, 415, 435, 466
HELYE 216
HEN(D)LEY 480, 489
HERNE 396
HERON 60, 61, 490
HETHE 350
HEWET 402
HINXHILL 310
HIXE 225
HOBALL *64*
HOBBES *65, 66*
HOLE 180
HOLMAN 55, 64
HOLMES 50
HOLT 358
HOLTBIE 29
HOMES 234
HOPPER 353, 481
HORDEN 213
HORLOCKE 168
HORSLYE 378
HORWOOD 9
HOWES 224
HOWLYN 158
HOWSOLEY *64*
HUBBARD 485
HUDSON 221
HUGH 434
HUMFRY 402
HYETT 460
HYNXWELL 173

ICKHAM 42, 472
IDEN 441
INWOOD 249

JAMES 6
JEFFEREY - see GEFFRY
JOHNSON 192
JOLL 150
JOMPE 497
JONES 258
JOYE 472
JUDSON 428
JURDEN 71

KELSHAM 174

KENSHAM 337
KETE 267
KEVILL 246
KIRRYE (-EY) 59, 71
KNOTTS 466
KNOWLES 388
KYNGSDOWNE 273
KYTHERELL 335
LACY 479
LAKE 270, *64*
LANE 339
LANG(E)LEY 63, *64*
LAUNDER 183
LAWE 409
LEEDES *64*
LEWES 410
LIVEROCKE 377
LODGE 257
LONDON 452
LONG(E) 381, 474
LONGELEY 365
LOO 498
LOVELACE 93
LOWE 439
LUCAS 268
LYLLY 453
LYNCH 138, 486
LYNLEYE 388

MABYE 438
MAISTERS - see MASTERS
MALLOM 439
MALLYNSON 442
MAN 386
MARLETON 238
MARSH (MERSHE) 188, 266
MARTYN 320
MASON 334, 442
MA(I)STER(S) 251, 268, 464
MATHUE 179, 416
MAYNARD 475
MECOTT 277
MERCER *64*
MERSHE - see MARSH
MERYWETHER 293
MILLER (MYL-) 71, 406
MO(O)RE 465
MOS(S) 336, 408
MOSWELL 395, 410
MOUNT (MOWNTE, AMOUNTE) 360, 390, 473, *65, 66*
MUNGEN 191
MUSCULUS *11*
MYLLER - see MILLER
MYLLINGE 376
MYLL(E)S (MYLES) 217, 227, 283, 437, 458
MYLNER 226

MYNGE 315

NASH 471
NEAME 453
NETHERSOLE 312, 391, 409
NEVILL 1
NEVINSON *3(2)*
NEWSTREETE 447
NICHOLAS 203, 351
NORBERYE 404
NORDEN 205, 382
NORGRAVE 424
NORTON 77, *64*
NOTT 294
NOWER 262
NYCOLSON 425
NYNNE 455, *83*

ODYARNE (ODYAM) 447
OGAR - see AWGOR
OKELEY 47
OLIVER - (OLYVER) 248, 446
OVERY 359, 419
OWEN 279, 308

PACKHAM 195
PAGE 334
PAINE 348
PALMER *65, 66*
PANTRY 311, 328
PARDEW 482
PARKER Archbp *8*
PARRETT 451
PASHE 45, 81
PATYNDEN (PATTINDEN) 228, 383
PAWLEN 275
PEAKE 274
PEERNE 330
PEERS 383
PEREN 202
PEROTT 56
PERRY 301
PETENDEN 53
PETER 314, 374.
PETT 286
PETTYT 489
PHILLIPS 126
PICKERING 156
PLOMER 114
POLLARD 272
POTTEN (-YN) 325, 387
POTTET (-TYTE) 426, 441
POWELL 413, 460
PYBORN(E) 52, 498
PYLLING 214
PYNE 361

THE QUEEN (see also Injunctions in Index of Subjects) 4, 78, 262, 358

QUEEN MARY 77, 139, 141, 222, *29*, 360
QUESTONBURYE 232
QUIDLER 491

RADE 228
RAMESDALE 472
RAMYSE 468
RAND 281
RANDALL 479
RAWKYNS 437
RAWLYNS 47
REDAR *64*
REDESDALL 476
REIGNOLD 413
REP 78
REVELL 343
REYMET 462
ROBERT(ES) 269, 330
ROBSON 235
ROBYNSON 212
ROLF 290
ROPSON *64*
ROWE 474
ROYDON (-TON) 206, 236
RUSSELL 86
RYCHARD(S) 193, 460, 479
RYDLEY 231
RYGDEN 312

SAARE 350
SACRY 221
SANDY 403
SAUNDER(S) 338, 405, 451, 475
SCHERPE *64*
SCUDDER 411
SEKS 331
SENOKE 432
SHARP 471, 480
SHAWE 281
SHERMAN 334
SHIPTON 314, 374
SINCKLER 181
SINGLETON 366
SKAMBERLAYNE 420
SLODEN 312
SMETH 401
SMITH (SMYTHE) 167, 257, 260, 425
SMYTH(E)SON 233, 265, 295
SOLE 483
SPRACKLINGE (-YNGE) 291, 405
SPRIE 460
STACE *64*
STANDEN 361
STANFORD 404
STAPLE 381, 382
STARKY 363
STEDE 431

STERE (STIRE) 449, 450
STILE 453
STODDARD 132, 292
STONESTREETE 407
STRAUGHAM 153
STRETER 281
STRYCKLANDE 438
STUPPYN 473
STYNTON 219
SWETING 278, 375
SWETMAN 198, 471, *65, 66*
SYMPSON 157

TANNER 398
TATNALL 250
TAYLOR (TAI-, TAYLOURE) 172, 243, 284, 371
THOMAS - see APTHOMAS
THOMPSON 70, 83
THORNTON 431
TIPPING 471
TIRREY 419
TOFTS 410
TOLHERST(E) 400, 444
TOPLEY *64*
TOPPINDEN 324, 346, 380, 402
TORFET 431
TREVOR *64*
TRUSNOTHE 407
TUFTON 285
TURK 199
TURNER 210, 427, *64*
TYE 456
TYLLY 194, 285, 300

UNGLEY 430

VINCENT 229

WAGHORNE 228, 229
WALLBANCKE 489
WANDERTON *64*
WARD *65, 66*
WARDEN 443
WARE 78
WARNER 12
WARRYNER 44
WEBBE 319
WELBY 393
WELDYSHE 175
WELL(E)S 169, 252, 327, 344
WHETLAND 381
WHITFELD 304
WHYTE 264
WIGGSHILL (WYG-) 415, 435
WILSON 408
WOLF *64*
WOOD 280, 299, 359, 369, 413, 445, 496
WOTTON (WUTTON) 135, 347, 355
WRYGHT 477
WULGATE 298
WUTTON - see WOTTON
WYATT 476
WYCKS 242
WYGGSHILL - see WIGGSHILL
WYGMORE 218
WYLFORD 379
WYNCKE 190, 341
WYNTER 321
WYTHERDEN 455, *83*

YALE 459
YNGLAND 497
YNGLISHE 498
YORKE 479

INDEX OF PLACES

References in medium type are to item numbers, those in italics are to pages.

Alkham 151, 299
Appledore 401, 423
Ash 323
Ashford 69, 82, 124, 142, 157, 212, 223, 282, 377, 447, 449-451, 491, 495

Badlesmere 479
Bapchild 317
Barfreston 17
Barham 182, 238, 262, 305, 474
Bearstead 127, 396
Bekesbourne 93, 139, 301
Benchechilde 380
Benenden 110, 197, 228, 229, 267, 268, 485
Bethersden 285, 300, 407
Betnamswood 219
Betteshanger 123, 143
Biddenden 97, 219, 333, 334, 412, 448
Bilsington 49, 425, 431
Blean 283, 451
Bodiam (Sussex) 429, 479
Bonnington 3, 204
Borden 270
Boughton Aluph 399, 467
    Blean 67
    Malherbe 63, 88, 159, *64*
    Monchelsea 385, 464
Boxley *1*, 163, 357
Brabourne 14, 95, 134, 147, 460
Bredgar 270
Brenzett 398, 411
Bridge 233
Brook 140, 264
Brookland 79, 411, 433
Broomfield 76
Buckland by Dover 53
    by Faversham 129
Burmarsh 439

Canterbury *1*, 47, 323, 451, 476, 479, 482, *70*
    All Sts 280, 456
    Chapter House 455
    Christ Church 44, 205, 329, 344, 442, 451, 452
    Holy Cross 162, 190, 234, 254, 307, 341, 442, 443
    Hospital of Poor Priests 108
    Hospital of St. John 493
    Hospital of St Lawrence 493
    St Alph 261
    St And 42, 205, 250, 258, 395, 410, 424, 472
    St Dun 144, 155, 347, 355, 403, 442, 468
    St Geo 281, 314, 374
    St Gregory, monastery of 93
    St Mary Bredin 217, 308, 421, 422, 424, 472
    St Mary Bredman 214, 232, 424
    St Mary Magd 48, 54, 205, 460
    St Mary Northgate 235, 252, 339, 344, 349, 363, 438, 458, 460, 471, 487
    St Mild 68, 90, 179, 276, 413, 479
    St Mgt 15, 108, 249, 340
    St Paul 57, 121, 191, 196, 362, 460
    St Pet 280, 309, 310, 353, 410, 443, 471
    St Steph - See Hackington
Capel 150
Challock 70
Charing 202, 318, *70*
Charlton 130, 315
Chart, Great 86, 212, 319
Chartham 117, 206, 236, 253, 376, 431
Cheriton 386
Chilham 70, 186, 206, 236
Chillenden 2
Chislet 192, 208, 299
Coldred 137
Cranbrook 240, 284, 336, 345, 394, 426, 428, 430, 437, 444, 445, 450, 459, 466, 469, 480, 481, 492
Crundale 122

Deal 171, 198, *65, 66*
Doddington 89, 91, 288
Dover *1*, 476
Dymchurch 356
Eastchurch 273
Eastling 153
Eastry 26
Eastwell 172, 194
Elham *21*, 312, 473
Elmsted 1, 60, 61, 105, 148, 482, 490
Elmstone 73
Ewell 297, 358
Eythorne 216, 293, 296

Faversham *1*, 77, 222, *30*, 365, 384, 389, 477
Flimwell (Sussex) 412
Folkestone 454, 457, 461
Frittenden 428, 434, 435, 466
Godmersham 70
Goodnestone by Faversham 67, 83
Goudhurst *1*, 213, 269, 383, 432
Guston 5, 53, 479

Hackington 220, 378
Halden 446
Halstow 94, 397
Harbledown 185, 343, 378, 451, 455
   Hospital 493
Hardres, Lower 233
Hardres, Upper 20, 128, 265, 266, 295, 473
Harrietsham 12, 113, 375, 393
Hartlip 178, 278, 303, 375
Hastingleigh 14, 87
Hawkhurst 361, 444, *64*
Headcorn 173, 174, 221, 325, 330, 335, 338, 346, 400, 402, 475
Hinxhill 431
Hope 146
Horton 263, 360, 390, 460, 483
Hothfield *64*
Hythe 112, 158

Ivychurch 66, 209, 286, 287
Iwade 259

Kenardington 24, 324, 380, 406
Kennington 21, 64, 166, 223
Kettenten in Nonington 296
Kingsdown 331
Kingsnorth 23, 496
Kingston 312

Langdon, Abbey of 4
Langdon, East 188
Langdon West 4
Leeds 126
Lenham 11, 18, 20, 300, 342
Lewes (Sussex) 465
Leysdown 16, 51
Linton 111, 175, 207
Littlebourne 58, 289
London 175, 474, 477
   St. Bride 413
Loose 207, 492
Lydden 154
Lyminge 282, 312, 328
Lynsted 78, 104, 381, 382

Maidstone *1(2)*, 434, 451
Marden *1*, 96, 199, 435
Mersham 260, 327

Milton by Sittingbourne 13, 409
Minster Sheppey 65, 306
Minster Thanet 436
Mongeham Gt. 498
Murston 84

Netherfield (Sussex) 466
Newington by Sittingbourne 395
Newenden 337, 429, 437
Newnham 114, 350
Newhaven (Sussex) 179
Nonington 170, 296
Northbourne 181, 187
Northiam (Sussex) 379

Orlestone 203, 425
Ospringe 55, 277
Otterden 115
Patrixbourne 452
Petham 164, 165
Postling 116, 141
Preston by Faversham 19, 56, 131, 145, *30*
Preston by Wingham 75, 177, 479

Queens Chapel 47

Rainham *1*, 408, 427
Reculver 192, 200, 208
Ringwould 52, 302
Ripple 302
River 133, 149, 476
Robertsbridge (Sussex) 465
Rodmersham 10
Rolvenden 62, 72, 241, 387, 388, 426, 441, 445
Romney, New 43, 45, 81, 160, 380, 433
Romney, Old 494, 497
Ruckinge 59, 71, 211, 225, 322

St. Mary in the Marsh 6, 22, 106
Sandhurst 102, 109, 118, 379, 429, 430, 465, 479
Sandwich 323, 453
Seasalter 135, 404, 486
Selling 156, 489
Sevington 46
Shadoxhurst 50, 66
Sheldwich 25, 99, *30*
Shepherdswell 101, 132, 292, 293, 297, 352
Sholden 274
Sittingbourne 84, 462, *70*
Smarden 7, *64*
Snargate 167, 494
Snave 478
Stalisfield 136, 298, 364
Staplehurst 85, 434
Stelling 20, 290
Stodmarsh 279

Stone in Oxney 98, 201, 226, 316
Stowting 294, 360
Sturry, 100, 224
Sutton by Dover 53, 80, 119
Sutton, East 161, 168
Sutton Valence 92, 161, 332

Tenterden 183, 184, 271, 391, 463,
    488, *64*
Teynham 321
Thanet, St John 138, 329, 348
    St Lawrence 275, 329, 373, 405
    St Pet 291
Thanington 410, 455
Throwley 189, 359
Tilmanstone 304

Ulcombe 8, 120
Upchurch 193, 440, 470

Waldershare 216
Walmer 311
Waltham 320
Warbleton (Sussex) 445
Warden 103
Warehorne 203, 218, 239, 351, 354
Westbere 215
Westwell 484
Whitstable 210
Willesborough 251, 255, 257, 268,
    431, 467
Wingham 125, 169, 313
Womenswold 152, 272
Woodnesborough 74, 176, 180, 453
Wootton 262
Wormshill 9
Worth 26
Wychling 195
Wye 227, 256, 326

INDEX OF SUBJECTS

absolution, text of 459
abuse (and see railing) 86, *41,* 352-355, *68, 73*
accounts defective or wanted 226-228, 230, 232, 233, 381, 352
act book *4*
adultery 71, 402, 442-460, *73, 75*
alb 228, *81*
'Alcuin Club Collections, *3(2), 4, 6, 18, 68*
ale hunters 243, 371, *68*
altar or Communion table (and see cloth, altar) 269, *69*
ambulation 60
'Annals of the Reformation' *8*
apparel of minsters (and see alb, gown, surplice) *68*
apparitor 159, 194, 427
apprentices 214 ,*81*
Arches, Court of 453, 455
Archbishop's register *6*
archdeacon (and see Official) *1*
arrangement of the book *6*
articles, Visitation — see Visitation
Royal *3*
assault in church 234, 238

banns of marriage 42, 384-388, 405, 408, 409, 471, 472
baptism (and see christening) 235
barley, gifts of 302, 304, 305
bastardy - see fornication, adultery
bawdry 480, *61*
beads, wearing of 249, *68, 74*
bell, tolling or ringing of 26, 256, 485
bells stolen 486
benifices - see fruits
Bible lacking or defective 128, 129, 131, 135, 139, 141, 142, 72
    portions to be learnt by clergy *71*
    provision of *68*
bigamy 65, *41,* 469-479, *73*
blasphemy and swearing *41,* 347, 350, 351, 363-365, 444, *73, 75*
bond 201
bonfire 491
books lacking (see also Bible, Paraphrase, psalter, homilies) 26, 129, 130, 137, 141, *72*
    of Queen Mary's time 77-79, 139, 250, 251, 254, *71, 76*
bowling - see gaming
brawling 234, 241, *73, 78*
bread for Communion (and see holy loaf) 73-76, *69, 82*
    'Wassall bread' for the poor 292

breviary - see books of Queen Mary's time
buggery 73
burial (and see funeral)
    fee for 353
burning 481-483, *74*

candles *68*
Canterbury - see diocese
    Prerogative Court of 382
'Canterbury Administration' *3*
cap, wearing of 89-90
cards (playing) - see gaming
Catechism 5, 18, 40, 41, *69, 71, 72, 81*
causes ex officio - see office causes
    instance - see instance
    testamentary *2(2)*
    matrimonial *2*
    tithe *2*
    payment of church rates etc. *2*
    church seating *2*
    faculties *2*
    slander *2*
ceremonies *68*
chalice or Communion cup 129, 130, 143-155, 311
chancel, repair of - see repairs
chancel steps 127
Chapter - see General Chapter
charms 253
chasuble 228
chest, parish 124, 129
child, illegitimate - see fornication, adultery
choir 222, *74*
christening, irregular 58, 212, 213, *74*
church and chancel, separation between 104
church, attendance at (and see Communion, receiving) 26, 44, 162, *25,* 190-225, 234, 370, *68, 73, 75, 79*
church, failing or neglecting to attend, 22, 156-225
church in ruins 103
church, repair of - see repairs
church property, witholding of - see withholding
churching of women 213, 417, 436
churchwardens, duties of *2,* 226-229, 232, *41, 73*
churchyard, fencing or enclosing of 113-116, *72*
    keeping swine in 308
    made pasture 315
clerk, parish - see parish clerk
clergy, analysis of *70*
    failure in duty of *9,* 17-58, *72*
    lack of *8,* 2-5, *12, 72*

clergy misbehaviour of *12, 59-71, 72*
clergy - see also non-residence, plurality
cloth, altar or Communion table 129, 313
    front 226
    Lent 226
Commandments, Ten 19, 28, 30, *68*
Common Prayer, Book of (and see books) *79*
Commissary *1*
Commissioners, Queen's 256
'Commonplaces of Christian religion . . .' *11*
communicants, return of number of 5
Communion table - see altar
Communion, receiving 41, *22,* 156-189, *71, 73, 75, 81, 82*
    giving 17, 28, 29, 34-36, 43, 69, 78, 80
    at marriage 392, 393
Communion cup - see chalice
Communion table (and see altar) 119, 129
comperta - see detecta
compurgators 5
'Consistory Court of the Diocese of Gloucester, The' *1*
contumacy *4*
cope 228, *81*
Court of Arches 453, 455
courts, Working of the *1*
cows, gift of 266, 293, 294, 296, 298-300
    value of 294, 298
Creed 19, 30, 350, *68*
cross, carrying of at burials 255
cruets 127

dancing in time of Divine Service 231
Dean (Rural) *71*
death penalty *38*
deceiving the Court 497
detecta et comperta *2, 5*
    analysis of *72-74*
dice - see gaming
diocese of Canterbury, extent of *1*
directions to clergy (and see Injunctions) *3*
dirge, gift for 272, 273
disciplining of private lives *41*
Divine Service - see dancing, playing, victualling in time of,
    defects in or lack of 26, 37-38, 61, *72*
    disturbances of 235-237, 239-241, 349, *68, 78*
    banning of 84
divorce 408
doctrine 239
'drag' 308
drunkenness (and see ale hunters) 61, 366-370, 372, 444, *73, 75*

eavesdropper 339
'Ecclesiastical Law' (Burn) *5*
elders and betters, respect for 498

'Elizabethan Religious Settlement, The' *6*
ember days 57
evil livers *81*
ewes (or sheep), gift of 265, 295, 297, 298, 301
    value of 297, 298, 301
excommunication *4, 5,* 32, 51, 58, 69, 70, 157, 158, 167, 171, 180, 190-193, 221, 223, 281, 284, 287, *38,* 320, 322, 324, 325, 327, 334, 338, 347, 357, 375, 403, 404, 406, 407, 410, 412-414, 419, 420-423, 426, 431, 434, 435-437, 439, 440, 443-446, 449-451, 453-455, 458, 459, 461, 463, 464, 468, 469, 472, 475, 478, 485, 492, 494, 496, *83*
Excommunication, text of sentence *83*
executors (or administrators), bequests withheld by - see gifts by will
    neglect of duty of 41, 373-382, *73*
exempt parishes, *3, 18, 70*
exhibitions for scholars 382, *68*

farmer of parsonage *8, 9,* 31, 49, 132
fautors of usurped power *68*
feasts, celebrating unlawfully 257, 258
fees *12*
    collection of *2*
felony *38*
fines *6*
forfeiture for non-attendance at church 207, 218-220, *79*
fornication 428-35, 443, 497, *73, 75*
fortune telling 253
fruits of benefice, distribution of 31, 33, *68*
funeral service 81-82, 255
furnishings, church *18,* 117-155, *21, 72*

gaming 59, 61, *72*
General Chapter *3, 5,* 120, 455
gifts by will 275, 276, 278, 281, 282, 291, 314, 317, 373-380, 383
gifts to poor - see poor, gifts to
gifts for repairs of roads etc - see repairs to roads
goods of persons deceased (and see gifts by will) *71*
gown, black 80
grain 302-5

handwriting vi, *5*
harbouring a suspected person 414-420, *73, 74*
heresy *38, 68*
highways, bequests for - see repairs to roads etc.
holy days *68*
holy loaf 303

94

homilies, book of *18*, 129, 137, 138, 140, *68*
   failure to read 25
Hospital of St. Lawrence 493
   Harbledown 493
   St. John 493
hospitality, keeping by clergy 10
household, responsibility for 181, 215-217

idiot 224
idolatry - see images etc, monuments
ill ('yvill') rule 346, 368, 408, 410
images etc 56, 126, 127, 251, 261, *68(2)*, *71, 76*
imprisonment *6*, 172, 197
incantations - see witchcraft
incest, *41*, 461 -468, *74*
incontinence 421-427
induction, certificate of 2, 51
Injunctions - see directions to clergy
   Royal *4*, 27, 33, *18*, *25*, 203, 293, *68-9*
Inquisition, The *38*
'instance' causes ('to proceed according to law') 2, *34n*, 275, *37n*, *41*, 434
institution, certificate of 2, 14, 51
'Introduction to Ecclesiastical Records, An' *1*

Jurisdiction, area of *1*
   exemption from *3*

Lambeth Palace Library *6*
lamp or light, gifts for *32*, 262-271, 299
land, gifts from 267-272, 274-276
lantern 226
lenocinium 496
libri cleri *2, 3*
licence to preach *2, 68*
   for marriage 48, 390
   to serve cure 52
   to midwife 487
   to teach *68*
'Life and Acts of Archbishop Parker' *8*
lights, gifts for maintenance - see lamp
Litany, The *68, 69*
City of London Grammar School 382
Lord's Prayer (Paternoster) 19, 28, 30, *68*

magistrates, fear of by clergy 39
maintenance of illegitimate child 434, 435
market place (for penance) 323, 329, 426, 428, 434, 445, 450, 451, 476
marriage, irregular 42, 45-48, 54, 63, *41*, 384-394, 471, 472, 73
   prohibited period for 45, 46
   out of the parish 389-391, *74*
   place unknown 394
   partners living apart 68, 395-402, 449, 473, 474, *73*

marriage, precontract of 427
   of clergy *68*
Mary - see Queen Mary
mass, gift for a 272
mass book - see books of Queen Mary's time.
meat, eating on fast days 77
'Medieval Ecclesiastical Courts in the Diocese of Canterbury' *3*
midwife 213, 415, 420, 487
minstrel 225
miracles 56
misbehaviour of the clergy *12*, 59-71
   of laymen 339-372
monition in place of penalty *6*
monuments etc, destruction of (and see images) 126, 127, 260, *71, 76*

non-residence of clergy *2, 9*, 6-10, *12*, 15, *72*, *75, 76*
   dispensation for 9

obit 268
occupations (lay)
   butcher 365
   glover 370
   miller 245
   sawyer 477
office causes *2*
Official of archdeacon *1, 2*
orders, letters of *2*
ornaments of the church (and see furnishings, images, monuments) 130, *80*
overseers for attendance at church 221, 231
   of the poor *41*

papal bull *38*
Paraphrase of Erasmus *18*, 129, 131-134, 136, *68, 72*
parish clerk, appointment of 85
   misbehaviour of 233
   wages of 306-308
parents and masters, duty of 214, *81*
'parson' *8*
paten *21*, 311
Paternoster - see Lord's Prayer
parsonage in decay - see repairs
patrons *8, 72*
penalties inflicted *5*
penance *5*, 29, 36, 178, 201, 323, 329, 364, 411, 413, 415, 420, 426, 428, 433-435, 442, 445, 450, 451, 452, 457, 458, 460-462, 464-466, 472, 476, 478, 479, 485, 494, 496-498
   commutation of 42, 420, 435, 452, 460, 464
perambulation 60, *68*, 75
pigeon house 107

pilgrimages *68*
'place libera me' 81
playing in time of Divine Service 246
pledging church silver 153
plurality *9*, 6-8, 11-14, 16, *70, 72*
    dispensation for 9, 13, 14, 16
poor, gifts to (and see poor box) *6*, 32, *29*, 268, 276, 278-293, 373-375, *74*
poor box or chest 42, 121, 123, 281, 306, 366, 435, *68*
poor, rate for 288-290
poor maidens married, gift for 314, 373, 374
popery 56, 148, *31*, 249-261, *72, 73, 76*
portes (portuis) 78
prayer, reverence at *69*
prayers' 'little book of *20*, 138
preaching - see sermons
presentments *2, 4, 7, 41*
prickets, gift for 296
prison - see imprisonment
processionals (book) *72*
psalms, singing of 254
psalter 133, 137
pulpits *18*, 123, 125, *68*
'purcyfannte' 330
purgation *5*, 64, 71, 171, 219, 252, 259, 261, 320-329, 339, 341, 343-345, 347, 357, 362, 363, 368, 372, 403, 406, 407, 410, 413, 421, 422, 425-427, 438, 443, 446, 447, 449, 453-458, 463, 467, 480, 490
purgation doubled 453, 456

Queen Mary *3n*

railing (and see scold & unquiet) 339, 343-345, *73*
readers *8*, 3, 40, 49, 50, 479, *70, 72*
'Readers and Sub-deacons, Report to the Convocation of Canterbury' *8*
reading desk 125
reconciliation 29, 69, 182-189, *68, 81*
'Records of the Established Church of England, The' *1*
references, explanation of 7
register (parish) *68, 71*
    lost 55, 124
relics 56
relief from parsonage 316
repairs, cost of 99-102
repairs materials for
    glass 92, 98, 99, 102
    lead 102
    shingling 99
    stone 92, 107
    tiling 99, 107
repairs, rate for 101, 111, 114, 279, 280
repairs to chancel 1, *16*, 91-97, 102, *72*

repairs to church *16*, 98-102, 111, 278-280, 313, *72*
    to parsonage or vicarage 105-110
    to churchyard (and see churchyard, fencing of) 111, 112, *72*
    to roads etc. 277, 376, 377, 379, 383
    to steeple 100, 101
    to tombs 492
'Report of the Lower House of Convocation 1885, no. 183' *3*
rochet *81*
rood loft, removal of *18*, 117, 118, *72*
rubrics *81*
ruffs and breeches, speaking against 354

School, City of London Grammar 382
Sabbath, working on the (and see Divine Service) 369
schoolmaster 488, *74*
scold (common) or railer 241, 347-349, 357, 363, *73, 75*
seditious books *69*
selection for this book, basis of *6*
selling or taking church goods (and see witholding church property) 226-229
sequestrators accounts 230, *71*
sermons, lack of 20-24, 34, *72*
    complaint of 86-88, 136, 354, *72*
servant, desertion of 489
Service - see Divine Service
'seve and sheres' (in witchcraft) 332
sexton 228, 229, 261
sexual offences *48-60*
sheep - see ewes
sidemen *2*
significavit' *6*, 434, 459, 495
silver, value of *18*, 155
simony 53, *68*
'Sir' as prefix to name *5*
singing in church 76, *69*
slander *41*, 339, 356-362, 365, 498, *69, 73*
sorcery - see witchcraft
spelling *5*
stocks, to sit in 476
stoup, holy water 127
superstition *64*, 259
surplice 82, 122, 128, 129, *81*
surrogate *1, 3*
suspicious living 62, 64, 66, *41*, 396, 403-413, *73*
swearing - see blasphemy

tabernacle 120
tables (playing at) - see gaming
talk, rash *68*
tapers, gifts for (and see torches) 263, 264
teaching, school 488, *68*
teller of tales *41*, 339, 340, *73*

testamentary causes *41*
timber, cutting of 67, 116, 313
    selling of 83
tithes 53, 309, 310, *68*
torches, gifts for 269
treason 360
tunic 228
uniformity *71, 79*
unquiet (disquiet) *41,* 341, 342, 459, *75*
usury 490

victualling in time of Divine Service 244, 246, *68, 73*
Visitation, Archibishop's *6,* 173, 174, 294, 390, 434
    articles *3*
    books *1*
    Metropolitical *6*
    Royal *6,* 44, 230, 261, *69*
    proceedure in *2, 3, 4*

'Visitation Articles and Injunctions' (Alcuin Club Collections) *3(2), 4, 7, 18, 68*
Visitations, list of *67*

wax, gifts of 271
wheat, gift of 303
whoredom 436-441
wife beating 484
will, gift by - see gifts
'Winchester Consistory Court Depositions 1561-1602' *1*
witchcraft (sorcery, incantations) 70, 171, 253, *38,* 318-338, *68, 73, 80*
witholding church property 230, 262-317, 375, *73*
working outside the parish 210, 211
writ 'de excommunicato capiendo (and see 'significavit') *6,* 193